A Toolkit for
Department Chairs

A Toolkit for
Department Chairs

Jeffrey L. Buller and Robert E. Cipriano

ROWMAN & LITTLEFIELD
Lanham • Boulder • New York • London

Published by Rowman & Littlefield
A wholly owned subsidary of
The Rowman & Littlefield Publishing Group, Inc.
4501 Forbes Boulevard, Suite 200, Lanham, Maryland 20706
www.rowman.com

Unit A, Whitacre Mews, 26-34 Stannary Street, London SE11 4AB

British Library Cataloguing in Publication Information Available

Library of Congress Cataloging-in-Publication Data Available

ISBN 978-1-4758-1418-7 (cloth : alk. paper)
ISBN 978-1-4758-1419-4 (pbk. : alk. paper)
ISBN 978-1-4758-1420-0 (electronic)

∞™ The paper used in this publication meets the minimum requirements of
American National Standard for Information Sciences—Permanence of Paper for
Printed Library Materials, ANSI/NISO Z39.48-1992.

Printed in the United States of America

Contents

Preface   vii

Acknowledgments   ix

Introduction   xi

1   Hiring and Evaluating Faculty Members   1

2   Mentoring Faculty Members   19

3   Promoting Teamwork and Collegiality   38

4   Communicating Effectively   56

5   Managing Conflict   74

6   Making Decisions   92

7   Budgeting   108

Epilogue: Our Reflections   127

Appendix A   129

References   131

About the Authors   133

Preface

Throughout a multi-year study of over 4,000 department chairs conducted by Robert Cipriano (one of the coauthors of this book) and Rick Riccardi (Associate Vice President for Institutional Effectiveness at Southern Connecticut State University), several findings have remained surprisingly constant. Each year only 3 to 4 percent of the department chairs who participate in the study indicate that they received formal training in how to do their jobs. Moreover, the remaining respondents—the overwhelming majority—are consistent about the type of training they feel they need the most. The following are the top seven answers in this extended study, ranked by the percentage of chairs who say they both want and need training in that area.

1. Evaluating Faculty   88.9%
2. Budgeting   81.4%
3. Communicating Effectively   77.9%
4. Managing Conflict   77.4%
5. Making Decisions   74.4%
6. Mentoring Faculty   69.2%
7. Promoting Collegiality   68.2%

While it would be wonderful if every administrator who wanted it could participate in a workshop on each of these topics, many chairs feel that they just don't have the time to set aside their responsibilities for prolonged training. So this book is intended to provide the next best thing: it's a toolkit of activities that department chairs can use to participate in their own administrative training when and where they want it. We cover the seven topics that chairs describe as their greatest needs, although you'll encounter these topics, not in order of priority, but in the way that most chairs actually encounter them: from hiring and evaluating faculty all the way through planning and defending effective budgets.

The department chair has become an increasingly important position in higher education. Many institutions find that nearly 80 percent of the decisions they make occur at the department level. As a result, an effective, skilled, and well-prepared body of chairs can make or break the success of a university. Nevertheless, the position is often poorly defined, and deans, faculty members, students, and even the chairs themselves may have unclear ideas of the role. While many faculty handbooks include job descriptions for chairs, every chair soon realizes that the responsibilities of the position go far beyond what's written in the manual. Moreover, higher education is changing rapidly, and the chair's role has continued to grow as a result.

What sort of person should institutions select to chair a department? Someone who is a successful grant writer? An internationally acclaimed scholar? A master teacher? From more than thirty years each of administrative experience at all kinds of academic institutions, we've concluded that: (1) There is no single "right" type of person to chair every department; (2) Most faculty members can be effective as chairs if they receive the proper training; and (3) Factual knowledge encompasses only a tiny fraction of what that training should be.

The most important factor in helping a faculty member become successful at departmental administration is thoughtful reflection on the choices academic leaders have to make every day. We've designed this book to provide abundant opportunities for you to reflect on those very issues. So no matter whether you're a prospective chair, a new chair, or an experienced chair, we think that there will be something in the pages that follow that can make your job easier, less stressful, and more satisfying.

Acknowledgments

The authors would like to thank, first and foremost, Patricia Mosto and Dianne Dorland, whose *A Toolkit for Deans* provided the blueprint for the current work. In addition, we are grateful to Sandy Ogden for her editorial assistance, and to the hundreds of participants in our workshops over the years with whom we field-tested many of these case studies.

We would like to acknowledge our editor, Tom Koerner, for his solid support throughout this project (including the fastest email reply we have ever received from an editor telling us that he liked our idea for a companion volume to *A Toolkit for Deans*). The entire staff of Rowman & Littlefield have been phenomenal.

Finally, we offer our thanks to our long-suffering spouses who have heard all our stories countless times and yet somehow always manage a smile when we trot them out yet again.

Introduction

Our favorite books when we were children were those featuring Donald J. Sobol's amateur detective Encyclopedia Brown. As the son of a police chief, Brown solved petty crimes and mysteries in his neighborhood using his "encyclopedic" knowledge and talent for noticing small details. Brown easily spotted factual errors or inconsistencies in forged documents, and he punctured the alibis of bullies, cheats, and thieves. Each Encyclopedia Brown adventure was only a few pages long, but it was filled with information, and as readers we were challenged to distinguish the important from the merely distracting and to hone our critical thinking skills by solving the mystery along with the hero.

If, after thinking long and hard about the mystery we still couldn't find the solution, all we had to do was to turn to the "Answers" section at the back of the book and learn how Encyclopedia Brown had saved the day. This format was great preparation for our future work as department chairs because it taught us to interpret information within a specific context, not just gloss over a text for its surface meaning. As long as we paid close attention to the details Sobol outlined, we, too, could spot the contradictions, draw logical conclusions from the information we received, and succeed in one situation after another. And if all else failed, the answers were always in the back of the book.

If only chairing a department were like that! If academic leadership were an Encyclopedia Brown mystery, the complexities we face in our jobs would be easily addressed and, when we couldn't figure out what to do, we'd simply go to the answers in the back of the book. But unfortunately, the real world of academic leadership doesn't work that way. Shades of gray are far more common than obvious solutions, and sometimes there *is* no right answer, just the best choice among a group of unfortunate alternatives. So although reflecting on case studies develops many of the same critical thinking skills that we learned as children from those Encyclopedia Brown mysteries, don't go looking for black-and-white "answers" in the back of this book. You won't find any.

The cases and scenarios you'll encounter in this book aren't brainteasers. They often don't have single solutions. Instead, some of them are problems that have no real answer at all, others are problems that have several different possible answers, and others have answers that address part of the problem but not the whole thing. In this way, they're just like the real situations you'll face day after day as a department chair. Often the approach you select when dealing with a challenge will depend on your own personality, situation, and institution.

A Toolkit for Department Chairs has been modeled to parallel Patricia Mosto and Dianne Dorland's *A Toolkit for Deans* (2014). In the chapters that follow, you'll find practical advice based on our own experiences as chairs and our observations of best practices in departments at a diverse range of colleges and universities. We've intentionally kept the advice sections brief because we know how busy you are. Besides, effecting departmental leadership isn't learned by reading about strategies and guiding principles. It's learned by applying those strategies and principles in real situations and seeing what works and what doesn't.

Case studies and scenarios provide a shortcut to that type of experience. As you read each situation we present, we encourage you to ask yourself the following questions:

- What process did I use to decide how I'd handle this challenge?
- Do I seem to be reverting to the same two or three processes again and again even though the situations I'm reading about are very different?
- If I decided to change my tactics on the basis of one or more of the questions that followed the case study or scenario, what were the factors that led me to choose a different approach?
- Did the case study or scenario seem to suggest any fundamental values that are guiding me in making my administrative decisions?
- If I were to develop a statement of my own philosophy of chairing a department, how could I incorporate some of the concepts I learned about academic leadership from this case study or scenario?

We really do intend *A Toolkit for Department Chairs* to be a practical set of tools that can help you become more effective in your administrative role. You can use the toolkit in many different ways. You can read through each chapter on your own, envision possible solutions to the cases and scenarios, and gradually hone your skills in dealing with various problems. You can discuss these cases with several other chairs, critiquing each other's solutions and learning as a group how each of you tends to handle the different problems that occur on the job. You can adopt *A Toolkit for Department Chairs* as a textbook for an academic leadership program, offered either by your own institution or through a professional organization, and use the challenges it poses as additional material to explore the techniques you're discussing in your training. You can use it as an assigned text if you're teaching a course like Higher Education Management, Problems in Higher Education Administration, or Educational Leadership at the College or University Level. Or you can be creative and take advantage of these case studies in a unique way that best suits your individual needs and goals.

The choice is yours but, no matter which approach you choose, by the end of this book we hope you'll find yourself filled with fresh, exciting ideas about how to put your academic leadership into practice. And if that happens, we'd love to hear about the interesting discoveries you've made!

Jeffrey L. Buller
jbuller@atlasleadership.com
Jupiter, Florida

Robert E. Cipriano
recipriano@atlasleadership.com
Madison, Connecticut

www.atlasleadership.com
October 15, 2014

1

Hiring and Evaluating Faculty Members

There are few things we do as department chairs that have such a lasting effect on our programs as hiring and evaluating faculty members. You can have the most innovative strategic plan, the best curriculum, and all the funding you desire, but if you don't have the right team in place, your department won't achieve its goals. Sometimes people think that an academic department is like any other random collection of people: a group whose talents can be graphed as a typical bell-shaped curve, with a few people who are very good or very bad at their jobs, a larger group of people who are moderately good or bad at their jobs, and a very large group of people in the middle, who are satisfactory but not particularly notable.

However, that scenario rarely occurs. If we do our jobs well when we hire and evaluate faculty members, our departments should have far more excellent and extremely good faculty members than those who are merely adequate or unsatisfactory. We may joke about Lake Wobegon, Garrison Keillor's fictional town "where all the women are strong, all the men are good looking, and all the children are above average," but in higher education the typical academic department is a place where "all the professors are above average." Our effectiveness in hiring and evaluating faculty members nearly guarantees it.

One of the most important tools chairs need in their toolkits, therefore, is skill in identifying potential faculty members who will be a good fit for the program and then, once the faculty members are hired, the ability to evaluate them fairly, objectively, and constructively in order to continue their professional growth. These skills are important, but they are not actually very difficult. You will be happy to know that a great deal of successful hiring and evaluation is simply a matter of ordinary common sense. For example, here are a few important guidelines to keep in mind when making hiring decisions:

- *Broaden people's vision.* Even if you're not a formal member of the search committee, as chair you have an important role to play in making sure that the process is fair and that the best possible candidate is chosen. In certain cases, you will want to urge the search committee from the very start not to develop a position description that is excessively narrow. For example, if the academic specialty required in the announcement is too limited or the amount of experience required in teaching specific courses is too high, you may end up excluding some very desirable candidates from the pool who could be an excellent fit for your program. Urge the search committee to list as requirements only those qualifications that are absolutely necessary. Particularly if diversifying the department is an important consideration during this search, it is unwise to create a job description that could unintentionally exclude candidates from currently underrepresented groups.
- *Search for fit, not perfection.* When screening applicants, try to keep the search committee focused on the right balance between the applicants' credentials and their potential fit in the department. As a general rule of thumb, search committees tend to hire candidates on the basis of their credentials, but faculty members succeed or fail on the basis of their fit. An applicant with a degree from an Ivy League institution may appear to be the best choice on the basis of academic preparation, but if that faculty member is not a good colleague, does not assume his or her fair share of the department's responsibilities, and refuses to teach the courses most necessary for the program, that person will not seem to have been the wisest choice two or three years later. If you burrow down into the issues raised by the questions "What do we really *need* from the person who will occupy this position? What are we currently missing, not simply in terms of academic specialties, but also skills and attributes? What sort of person will be the best colleague for us in the years ahead?" you are far more likely to develop the applicant pool you really want.
- *Trust your instincts.* If as chair you have the opportunity to select which candidate to hire or to recommend a limited list of finalists to the dean, the same issues that have guided your conversations with the search committee will also be important in making your

selection. Try not to let qualifications that make a candidate superficially impressive override your concern about more fundamental issues. At times, it can be important simply to trust your instincts. If something does not seem right about a candidate or gives you an uneasy feeling, you may be picking up on a quality that could potentially cause problems later. Remember that people are always on their best behavior during an interview. Even aspects of the candidate that were only mildly irritating or unsetting when you were with the person for a single day could be signs of major character defects that become much more apparent once the person is on the faculty.

For more about the chair's role in working with faculty searches, see Buller (2012), 157–87.

CASE STUDY 1.1: WHOM DO YOU HIRE—AND WHY?

Let's try applying these principles by exploring a case study. For our first exercise of this kind, you do not have to stretch your imagination too far. Your role is that of a department chair in your own discipline at your own university. (In other words, your role for this case study may be the job you actually have right now.) Imagine that a search for a new assistant or associate professor has been conducted, and a deadlock has occurred over which of two finalists the committee should recommend. You were unfortunately away at a conference during the interviews and have only the following summary of each candidate's strengths and weaknesses.

But you have one major concern: after many years of advocating for another full-time faculty position, your dean has only somewhat reluctantly approved this search. You are fearful that if you do not hire one of these two finalists you will lose this much-needed position. Each of the two finalists has worked at two other universities for a combined total of nine years. With no other information to go on, which of the two candidates are you initially inclined to hire based on your program's needs, the applicant's likely fit with your institution, and your experience with what makes a faculty member successful in your discipline?

Table 1.1.

Candidate A	Candidate B
Average teacher	Good teacher
Great researcher	No refereed publications
Internationally known	Only locally known
Tolerates students	Liked by students
Record of success receiving grants	Never written a grant proposal
Perception of colleagues unknown	Letters of reference contain comments like "Great colleague!"

Questions

1. Since you have an option of bringing in that candidate as either an assistant or associate professor, which rank are you likely to recommend?
2. Would your decision be any different if any of the following were true about the candidate you otherwise would *not* have selected?
   a. He or she would add much-needed diversity to your program.
   b. He or she is a close friend of the president.
   c. He or she has a great deal of administrative potential and can easily be envisioned as a future chair, dean, or provost.
3. Would your decision be any different if your department were:
   a. Designated as one of your institution's most important programs in the strategic plan?
   b. Widely regarded as the weakest department at the institution?
   c. Generally regarded as academically strong but nearly dysfunctional because of internal conflicts?
4. Consider each of the following modifications to the table of strengths and weaknesses presented above. Do any of them make you change your recommendation?
   a. Both candidates are described as good teachers.
   b. While Candidate A is described as a "Good Teacher," Candidate B is described as a "Great Teacher!"
   c. Both candidates are described as great teachers.
   d. Both candidates are described as great teachers, but while Candidate B remains described as a great colleague, Candidate A is described as "Non-collegial, rude, uncivil, a poor colleague."

e. The collegiality of the candidates remains as listed in the table but, instead of never having written a grant, Candidate B has several proposals for possibly significant grant applications pending.

f. Everything else about the candidates remains the same as in the table, but now both candidates are described as great researchers.

Resolution

As in all the case studies and scenarios in this book, there are no right or wrong answers. We will often supply you with a possible or recommended answer in the "Resolution" section of the case study, but even these suggestions should never be regarded as perfect "solutions." Particularly in the current case, your own situation will probably determine how you choose to proceed. If you are a chair at a community college or an institution where the teaching mission far outstrips the importance of research, it is likely that you will always prefer Candidate A whenever his or her evaluation for teaching is better than that of Candidate B. When they are ranked equally in teaching, the importance you place on the other qualities should reflect the needs and nature of your institution.

For example, you may be in a very large department or at a school where, because it covers a large geographic area or offers a majority of its programs online, faculty members rarely interact with one another. In that case, not knowing about Candidate A's collegiality—or even knowing that he or she is widely regarded as a poor colleague—may not be a large factor in your decision. On the other hand, if you are in a program that has already suffered numerous breaches of collegiality or is such a close-knit group that the presence of an uncivil faculty member would be highly disruptive, Candidate A's record in this area may make you highly reluctant to take a chance on his or her application.

In a similar way, if you work at a research university where the success of faculty members stands or falls on the basis of their scholarship, Candidate B's lack of publications and successful grant applications will almost certainly make you reluctant to extend an offer. When faced with the modification in which Candidate B is described as having several "significant" grant applications pending, your decision may depend on such factors as how important grant funding is to your program, your own risk tolerance (since those grants are only pending, not guaranteed), the relative importance of refereed publications versus grant support in your field, and how the factors of collegiality and teaching effectiveness fit into your overall needs.

This situation may be one in which you simply have to trust your instincts. Selecting the right faculty member is never an exact science anyway, and neither choice you make is guaranteed to be the correct one.

CASE STUDY 1.2: DON'T TELL MY BOSS!

You are the chair of a department that has "concluded" a nationwide search for a full-time faculty member at the rank of associate professor. A candidate who otherwise is at the very top of your pool of applicants insists that you cannot under any circumstances contact his current department chair or dean. Although you press the candidate on this issue, he or she refuses to give you a reason why. The candidate pool contains very few other applicants who are acceptable, and none of them even approach this candidate in the quality of their credentials. What do you do?

Questions

1. Do you:
   a. Contact the candidate's current department chair or dean, even though you were requested not to?
   b. Contact a prior chair or dean of the candidate who is not on the reference list provided but whom you were able to identify through an Internet search?
   c. Contact the candidate's current colleagues who are not on the official contact list but whom the candidate did not explicitly forbid you to contact? (In this case, you would be violating the spirit of the applicant's request but not its letter.)
   d. Offer the position to the next best candidate?
   e. Allow the search to fail?
   f. Do something else?
2. Does your answer change if:
   a. You knew for certain that you would lose the position if you did not hire someone from the current pool?
   b. The search were not for an associate professor but for an entry-level instructor or assistant professor?
   c. The rank of associate professor included automatic granting of tenure upon hiring?
   d. You had read in *The Chronicle of Higher Education* that there were ongoing tensions between faculty members and administrators in the candidate's college?

    e. One of your faculty members knew the candidate in a previous position ten years ago and tells you, "From what I knew then, this person seems like a good fit for us. There shouldn't be a problem."

Resolution

You decide that the candidate's unwillingness either to let you contact current supervisors or to give you a compelling reason for withholding this permission is just too much of a red flag. You proceed to the next qualified candidate who, although not possessing credentials nearly as stellar as your first-choice candidate, is perfectly capable of doing the job, lacking in any apparent "skeletons in the closet," and a good fit for the program. Your decision meets with some initial faculty resistance because there are those who believe the department has now lost its opportunity to bring in a candidate who could really put the program on the map. By the end of the new faculty member's first year, however, this controversy seems like ancient history. Your department's new member has become an accepted part of the community and has proven to be a good fit with your program. You are convinced that whatever you may have lost in terms of having a potential star on the faculty has been more than compensated for by the collegiality of the team you are building.

It is summer and most of your faculty members are away doing research or enjoying some time off. Your dean calls to tell you that another department at the university is trying to hire an internationally acclaimed scholar who will bring the institution several large grants, but who has a spouse who works in your academic discipline. The prestigious scholar will not accept the offer unless the spouse is also given a position with tenure.

To help close the deal, the dean is willing to give you a fully funded position for the faculty member's spouse, but you have to decide immediately whether you will accept the dean's offer. The problem is that the spouse is teaching in an area with declining student enrollments for which you already have four tenured faculty members who barely have enough to teach as it is. The spouse's course evaluations look satisfactory but far from excellent and, with the faculty away, you are unable to confer with them about what they would prefer.

Challenge Question: Do you accept this position that you do not actually need, risking the possibility of a faculty backlash because they were not consulted, or do you refuse the position, scuttling the search and risking the anger of the dean and the chair of the other department?

Scenario Outcome: Since the position does not cost your program anything, you would probably only refuse this position if the spouse's teaching evaluations were so bad that you believe the program would be harmed, your faculty was so sharply divided that contention over this decision would make the environment truly toxic, or you had reason to believe an untenured rising star was likely not to be renewed because your program would now be overstaffed. Although the scenario states that the spouse's academic area has recently been declining in enrollment, you are not given a reason why. It is possible that, with this new hire, fresh energy could be brought to the program. For this reason, you should probably accept the offer the dean is making.

Finding employment for qualified spouses of highly desirable candidates for faculty positions is increasingly an issue chairs must address during faculty searches. No one relishes the idea of being expected to fund a position for a candidate whom they did not select and may not particularly need. That reluctance is reduced, of course, when someone else is funding the position, and the new hire does not occupy one of the program's existing lines. As a chair, you have more leverage in situations in which the other program (as well as perhaps the dean and upper administration) is particularly eager to hire their preferred candidate. In that case, it is sensible to balance being a good team player with determining how your own program can benefit from the process.

LEADING FROM THE MIDDLE

Of course, chairs are not the only ones who make decisions when it comes to faculty hires. They are frequently acting on recommendations that have come to them from a search committee and then making their own recommendation to the dean, who makes the final decision. For this reason, department chairs frequently feel they are caught between two opposing sets of interests. In these cases, it is useful to try examining the matter from the perspective of the other person. What does he or she most want to happen and what is he or she most eager to avoid? If you can present

You are the chair of a highly collegial department of nine full-time faculty members, a close-knit group who enjoys one another's company both professionally and personally. At your institution, a departmental search committee makes a recommendation to the dean to hire a new faculty member. The established procedure is that the dean takes the search committee's recommendation under advisement, but the decision to hire is ultimately the dean's to make.

Your department has just completed a national search to hire an assistant professor and voted unanimously to offer the job to Dr. Seuss, who has two years of experience in a department very much like yours. However, the dean, who met all the finalists and reviewed the material, has decided to offer the position to Dr. Who, a candidate with a degree from a more prestigious institution who is currently completing a post-doc. The dean has met with the department and outlined reasons for this decision that you and your colleagues do not find persuasive. Everyone in the department, including you, still wants to hire Dr. Seuss.

Challenge Questions: How do you solve this dilemma? You do not want to appear weak to your faculty, but you also do not want to alienate the dean. Do you resign as chair on principle? Do you go along with the dean's choice? How do you placate your faculty?

Scenario Outcome: As you reflect on this situation, you decide that it is not a cause that warrants losing your position as chair. You meet with the dean and explain candidly why the department so strongly prefers Dr. Seuss and that they remain unanimously in favor of this candidate despite the arguments the dean had outlined during the meeting with them. You respectfully request that the department's recommendation be honored. If the dean accepts your reasoning, you will be gracious, thank the dean sincerely for listening to the views of the faculty, and refrain from characterizing this situation to the department as a victory over the upper administration.

"It was," you say when you announce the decision, "a collective decision among all of us because, on further reflection, the dean found our reasoning compelling and wants our program to succeed." If the dean still insists on hiring Dr. Who, you will not undermine this decision with the faculty. The choice of whom to hire is the dean's, after all, and you will devote your energy to making Dr. Who's arrival successful, not to licking your wounds or holding a grudge.

the proposal you want to adopt as a way of helping the other person get closer to his or her own goals, you will stand a far greater chance of having your plan approved.

For example, suppose you are persuaded by the argument of the search committee that the best candidate in a search is the one who has the strongest research record, while your dean and provost are always emphasizing the need for your program to increase its student credit hour production, retention and graduation rates, and scores on the National Survey of Student Engagement (NSSE). Rather than ignoring the interests of your supervisors and simply characterizing your request as a reflection of the faculty's will, find ways in which your preferred candidate can help the upper administration achieve its goals.

Since questions on the NSSE deal with how many students worked with a faculty member on a research project, completed a capstone project, learned to think critically, had experience in analyzing numerical or statistical information, or were exposed to complex real-world problems, you could argue that the candidate you prefer is actually the best possible choice for improving scores in this area.

You could begin looking for research demonstrating that students who engage in research projects under the direction of a faculty mentor are more likely to persist and eventually graduate. Along with your hiring recommendation, you could submit a proposed course rotation for the next two to four years that illustrates your plan for increasing student credit hour production across the department. In each case, you are helping your supervisor understand how achieving your own goals can be a way of helping that person achieve his or her own goals.

EVALUATING THE FACULTY

Once faculty members are hired, the chair's role shifts from seeking new people who offer *promise* of the best fit to mentoring those in the program so that they *perform* at their highest possible level. In annual surveys conducted of department chairs, evaluation of their colleagues is one of the duties that chairs consistently describe as among their least favorite. (See, for example, Cipriano and Riccardi, Winter and Spring 2014.) Part of the reason for this feeling—and one of the biggest challenges in conducting faculty evaluations effectively—is that this process causes chairs to balance three sometimes competing roles.

- *Supervisor.* At most institutions, the department chair is a line position with supervisory responsibility for the faculty. As such, the department chair needs to maintain the highest possible standards and hold faculty members accountable when they do not meet these expectations. The chair thus has the duty to be impartial when evaluating the faculty and to point out any instances in which their work has not reached the level of standards set for it. The required quality of the chair as a supervisor is *candor*.

- *Coach*. At the same time, a chair also has a responsibility to foster the development of his or her faculty. It can ruin morale to focus only on the negative or even characterize unsatisfactory work as an indictment rather than as an opportunity to improve. In order to mentor the members of the department, the department chair sometimes has to be highly diplomatic when discussing areas of weakness. The required quality of the chair as a coach is *encouragement*.

- *Champion*. Additionally, the chair is also the chief cheerleader for the program and its faculty and so must sometimes present its best appearance to the public. For example, suppose a department chair decides to recommend to the dean a faculty member's application for promotion that barely meets the criteria for that rank. Once the department chair has made the decision to send the recommendation forward, it is of no value whatsoever for the chair to waffle and draw attention to the candidate's weaknesses as well as his or her strengths. Once chairs decide to make a case for something, it is their job to make it as forcefully and effectively as they can. The required quality of the chair as a champion is *advocacy*.

CASE STUDY 1.3: THE LINE BETWEEN DUTY AND FRIENDSHIP

You are a tenured associate professor with twelve years of experience who is serving your first year as chair of a seven-member department. At your institution, chairs are elected by the department, and your election was vigorously contested; you received the position by only a single vote: your own. As a result, you have devoted a great deal of time to smoothing over any hard feelings people may have had.

Your best friend in the department, Dr. Affable, will be going up for tenure next year. You and your family often socialize with Dr. Affable, and the two of you carpool to work nearly every day. One day when Dr. Affable is away at a conference, another member of the department, Dr. Squealer, requests that an item of some importance be added to the agenda of that week's department meeting.

When the meeting reaches that point in the agenda, Dr. Squealer states that there are ongoing problems with Dr. Affable. He misses his classes frequently, his research has been minimal, and his students complain in private that he is a boring teacher. Rather than go through the upheaval of having a negative tenure vote the following year, Dr. Squealer recommends that Dr. Affable's contract not be renewed for the following year. At your institution, non-renewal of probationary faculty members is permitted, and you can still meet the timetable for doing so if you act quickly.

Dr. Squealer says at least four of the other six faculty members agree with him. He states that everyone knows the two of you are best friends but that they trust you to act with professionalism and integrity. He says openly that if you override the faculty's recommendation you will lose their confidence as the department's leader. What do you do?

Questions

1. Do you:
   a. Poll the faculty to see if Dr. Squealer is right about four others agreeing with him?
   b. Act as Dr. Affable's advocate?
   c. Try to determine what evidence Dr. Squealer has for his claims about Dr. Affable's poor performance?
   d. Decide that the opposition is too strong, Dr. Affable would lose the tenure vote in a year anyway, and so your best alternative is to issue a letter of non-renewal to Dr. Affable?
   e. Insist that the tenure decision will be made so soon that there is no need to act so precipitously?
   f. Stall for time and:
      i.   confer with the dean about a solution?
      ii. simply allow the deadline for issuing the letter of non-renewal to pass without any action on your part?
      iii. ask Dr. Affable what his own preference would be?
   g. Do something else?
2. Does your answer change if one or more of the following statements are true?
   a. Dr. Squealer was the other candidate for chair who lost to you by a single vote.
   b. You know that the dean is a strong supporter of Dr. Affable.
   c. Dr. Affable has privately confided to you that he is actively applying for other jobs and has several serious interviews at the conference he is currently attending.
   d. Dr. Affable is the only member of the department who has a physical disability.

An associate professor in your department will retire next year. As you look over her performance, you find problems everywhere you look. The students in her introductory courses often do very poorly in their more advanced classes. Her research, such as it is, has not consisted of anything more than an occasional book review or biographical entry for several years. Her colleagues dread serving on committees with her because she is so long-winded that they never make it through an entire agenda. You now have to write up her annual evaluation for her final year on the faculty.

Challenge Question: Do you handle this situation differently than you ordinarily would because the faculty member has already set a retirement date?

Scenario Outcome: First, you do some background work to make sure that the faculty member truly has committed to retire in a year and that there is no possibility she will extend her contract. Then you think, "What good will be served if I give her a harsh evaluation? She has been mentored in the past and has shown no improvement. If I am brutally honest, it will merely destroy her morale, and the students will be no better served. If for no other reason than her long commitment to the university, she deserves more humane treatment than that."

As a way of avoiding any possibility that the students will suffer for your leniency, you go to the dean to discuss an alternative assignment for the associate professor's last year. You find a task that is both valuable to the institution and within the faculty member's range of abilities. When you meet with the faculty member, you are neither unkind nor dishonest. You praise what you can, speak only in general terms about other areas of her performance, and gently explain to her the project you and the dean want her to complete during her final year on contract.

When she becomes a bit teary and says, "So you mean I'll never teach anymore?" you stress how important the project will be, the great need the institution has for the work to be completed within the coming year, and say, "This could be your legacy to the university. I want you to have this." Although you suspect she sees through your pretense, she accepts the assignment, and you conclude that you have handled the situation in a way that was both best for the students and respectful of the faculty member's dignity.

    c. Dr. Affable is openly gay, a lifestyle to which Dr. Squealer has previously objected on religious grounds.

Resolution

You tell the faculty that matters as serious as this one should not be decided as quickly as Dr. Squealer proposes. You note that the issue was added to the agenda only at the last minute and that you are concerned that the department will appear to be acting improperly by raising this issue while Dr. Affable is out of town. You mention evidence (assuming that you have any) that contradicts the perception that Dr. Affable is a poor teacher and researcher and note that, even if the faculty votes for non-renewal, making that decision is ultimately up to the chair. The meeting breaks up rather tensely, and you immediately discuss the situation with the dean who supports the way you handled the meeting.

Once Dr. Affable has returned from his conference, you fill him in on what happened at the meeting without attributing specific remarks to individual faculty members. Weighing the entire situation, Dr. Affable decides to accept an offer he received at the conference for another job. Until your conversation with him, he had been on the fence about the offer since the institution was located in a less desirable part of the country and the salary was not very competitive.

Given the entire situation, however, Dr. Affable decides that the other job is the best alternative he has at the moment. You are sorry to lose such a close friend, but you feel that you have handled a difficult situation in the best way possible.

CASE STUDY 1.4: EVALUATING ONE OR TWO?

You chair a department of six full-time faculty members. You have been at the university for thirteen years. One somewhat unusual aspect of your department is its homogeneity: both you and all your colleagues are tenured associate professors. One of them, Dr. Michele Thompson, is far and away the most productive researcher in your program. She has published extensively, receives many invitations to present at conferences, and serves as principal investigator on several grants. She is a popular teacher who is highly respected by peers, students, and staff members. Her achievements are so impressive, in fact, that she was awarded tenure after only three years at the university, an almost unheard-of occurrence for your program.

Michele's husband, Dr. Scot Thompson, is the department's only assistant professor, and he is currently being evaluated for tenure. He has not published any of his research, frequently cancels his classes to attend to personal business, serves on only one university-wide committee (meetings of which he has never attended), and has the reputation of being a poor colleague. People constantly describe Scot as an angry and arrogant young man with little to be arrogant about. In faculty meetings, you have heard him sarcastically dismiss the ideas of his colleagues, and course evaluations suggest that he conveys a similar attitude toward his students.

You were not inclined to evaluate Scot favorably for tenure anyway, but then you received a unanimous negative recommendation from the rest of the department. (Michele recused herself in accordance with your institution's policies.) The case seems very clear. But then, one by one, your faculty members stop by your office and say things like, "You know that if Scot goes, Michele will go, too," and "We just can't afford to lose Michele." You find yourself having to make a choice between losing someone who has been extremely valuable to the program and retaining someone who is already a problem and likely to become only worse after tenure. What do you do?

Questions

1. What is likely to be the result of taking each of the following actions?
   a. You meet with everyone in the department except Scot and Michele and tell them it is their decision to make. You outline the pros and cons of recommending Scot for tenure, take a secret ballot, and abide by whatever the result is.
   b. Since there are four faculty members in the program besides the Thompsons and yourself, the secret ballot comes back with two votes in favor and two votes against.
   c. You meet with other department chairs and solicit their advice.
   d. You meet with your dean, outline the situation, and ask for advice.
   e. You make a strong recommendation that the institution tenure Scot.
   f. You make a strong recommendation that the institution not tenure Scot.
2. Would your response be any different if any combination of the following were true?

a. You had it on good authority that the college-level committee would vote against tenure for Scot regardless of what the department recommends.
b. Scot were the only member of a severely underrepresented minority group in your college.
c. Scot had a physical disability.
d. Scot were the provost's brother.
e. Michele were the daughter of the chair of the governing board.
f. The provost had an unwritten policy of tenuring anyone the department recommended (even if that person were turned down at the college level) because "you're the ones who have to live with them, after all."
g. Michele had told you in confidence that Scot had been suffering from some health problems that caused him to miss classes, fall behind on his research, and respond irritably to other people. Those health problems are now fully treated, and Scot is likely to perform far better in the future.
h. You had an option to convert Scot's position to that of a non-tenure-track instructor, if he agreed.

Resolution

After giving the matter a great deal of thought, you decide that three important principles are at work here. The first is that, as wonderful as Michele is, no one is irreplaceable. If she decides to leave, you will have an opportunity to plan how to best use both her position and Scot's for the future development of the discipline. Perhaps your program would be better served by merging the two salaries and hiring one internationally known senior professor, splitting the two salaries into three instructor positions with heavy teaching loads so as to free up your other faculty members for additional research, or hiring two new entry-level assistant professors and redirecting the salary savings into additional funding for faculty travel. "Every departure is an opportunity," you recall one of your mentors saying, and the current situation appears to be a good example of how to apply that maxim.

The second principle at work is that you should never make the right decision for the wrong reasons. Just because Michele is a valuable addition to the department, it does not follow that you should do a disservice to your colleagues and students by retaining a faculty member with a clear record of ineffectiveness in teaching, research, or collegiality. The benefits that Michele brings could easily be outweighed by the damage Scot is capable of doing, and so tenuring him would be a very bad bargain indeed. You remember that, once Scot is tenured, it will be much more difficult for you to change his behavior or remove him from the institution if he proves incapable of improving his performance.

The third principle is that you should never assume you know what another person's decision will be. You learned this principle while conducting numerous faculty searches in which a member of the committee would say something like, "Oh, this applicant would never come here for this position. The pay's too low." or "Why would this candidate give up a tenured position for a job in which she'd just have to earn tenure all over again?" In several cases in which an offer was made anyway, the candidate in question eagerly accepted the position either because he or she had family members living in your area, was currently working in a very inhospitable environment, or had other reasons for liking your job better than his or her other prospects. In the same way, you decide that you're not going to make up Michele's mind for her. Although other faculty members *believe* she will leave if Scot does not receive tenure, you do not know that for certain and decide to take a calculated risk.

For all these reasons, you recommend that Scot not be granted tenure. The atmosphere in the department becomes filled with anxiety for a while, and Michele does *threaten* to leave, but she never actually does so. After a year and a half, Scot accepts a job at a local community college and begins to rebuild his career. Some time later, you run into Scot at a cocktail party and, to your surprise, he thanks you for giving him the "wake-up call" he needed. "If you hadn't set me straight, I never would have realized just how badly I was simply coasting on Michele's success. We're both much happier now, and the community college even decided to appoint me chair of the discipline. I guess I can count you as one of my mentors."

FOR REFLECTION

Hiring and evaluating faculty members are among the most important responsibilities of a department chair. Unlike the corporate world where underperforming employees can be dismissed at any time, colleges and universities pose unique challenges for ridding a program of an unsatisfactory faculty member. In systems where tenure exists, voiding the contract of a tenured faculty member is often a long and complex process.

Even when tenure is not an issue, it is extremely difficult to terminate a faculty member in the middle of a term because of the disruption it causes to the education of students and the continuation of research projects. For this reason, every hiring decision has to be made with great

Chapter 1

care. Screening applicants is an uncertain business: even people who look good on paper and interview very successfully will sometimes not live up to this initial promise. Effective evaluation processes are thus essential to help faculty members improve their performance and provide you with an early warning to possible problems.

2

Mentoring Faculty Members

Department chairs mentor their faculty members in both formal and informal ways. Formal mentoring is done when there is a clearly articulated arrangement between both parties about what the nature of the relationship will be, how often they will meet, what goals they will set, and how long the arrangement will last. Informal mentoring develops much more organically. Two people, one more experienced than the other, discover that they have a good rapport with one another, meet occasionally to talk about various issues related to their profession, and the senior member provides advice to the junior member as needed.

As department chairs, even if we happen to work at an institution that has not yet established a formal mentoring program, most of us have benefitted from both sides of the mentoring relationship. When we were just starting out, we probably regarded a more experienced member of our discipline as a role model and turned to this person whenever we had concerns or questions. Now that we are chairs, we almost certainly have had at least a few opportunities to advise new faculty members in our programs. Perhaps, too, we have served as mentors to new chairs in other departments. But no matter what our involvement with mentoring may be, doing it well is an important part of becoming a successful department chair.

While we may sometimes use the term "mentor" to embrace several different kinds of relationships, there actually are four different roles we need to distinguish in order to understand what is involved in a true mentoring relationship.

- A *confidant* is a person who listens to your concerns, providing comfort and support when your news is bad and experiencing genuine delight when your news is good. A confidant gives you an ear when you need to vent and a shoulder when you need to cry. Confidants rarely offer unsolicited advice and may even refrain from giving advice when you ask for it. Their job is to provide affirmation for you when you make a decision and to keep your secrets when you share them. The required quality of the chair as a confidant is *discretion*.

- A *sponsor* is a person who helps remove obstacles for someone else and works to advance his or her career. A sponsor puts you in contact with people you need to know and serves as your advocate when you need someone powerful in your corner. Sponsors may or may not meet with their protégés much in person. Their primary responsibility is to open doors for them that would otherwise be closed, and frequently that service is done via a phone call, letter, or private conversation held on their behalf. The required quality of the chair as a sponsor is *support*.

- A *coach* is a person who builds someone's skills and helps that person become more effective at performing a specific task. Although mentors may take on specific coaching duties from time to time, coaches may also be paid consultants who work with individuals to help them improve in such areas as public speaking, time management, strategic planning, and understanding organizational behavior. Their job is to critique the person's performance and provide instruction on how to perform even better. The required quality of the chair as a coach is *expertise*.

- A true *mentor* is a person who is able to draw on his or her own experience in order to assist someone's development. A mentor offers advice, wise counsel, and (when needed) reproof for actions that fell short of the mentor's standards. Mentors meet with their protégés on a schedule that suits them both and that reflects the specific nature of their relationship. Unlike sponsors, mentors do not always act as advocates for their protégés; they sometimes practice "tough love" by not protecting their protégés from the consequences of their actions. Unlike coaches, mentors are never paid for their services; the only compensation they receive is the satisfaction of having helped someone. Mentors know that both painful and pleasant experiences can be excellent learning opportunities. The required quality of the chair as a mentor is *wisdom*.

CASE STUDY 2.1: PROFESSOR PRIMADONNA

Three years ago you hired an extremely talented young faculty member—
Prof. Primadonna—who now leads your department in research productivity and receives excellent student course evaluations. It is likely that,
within a very short time, Prof. Primadonna will be nationally known as a
leading scholar in your field. There's only one problem. The rest of your
department absolutely *loathes* Prof. Primadonna. At first, you attributed
most of this reaction to professional jealousy.

Your department's junior faculty member was publishing more and
receiving larger grants than most of your senior faculty. In addition,
Prof. Primadonna is becoming increasingly popular with students who
love the professor's courses and recommend them to their friends. Yet
recently you've begun to understand why Prof. Primadonna has become
so widely disliked by the rest of the faculty.

You've noticed, for instance, that when other members of the department are greeting one another, Prof. Primadonna doesn't even bother to
say hello. When speaking to other faculty members, Prof. Primadonna
can be curt, even rude. The professor "doesn't suffer fools gladly," and
can be brutally frank when a colleague makes a suggestion that the professor regards as foolish or sends an email message that contains a typo-
graphical error. Prof. Primadonna feels free to ignore departmental duties
that "just aren't worth my time," and has recently handed off several
advisees to other faculty members because "they're not going to survive
in our program as majors anyway."

It is a departmental tradition that each faculty member in rotation takes
minutes at faculty meetings; Prof. Primadonna has refused to take a turn
as secretary. When challenged about this behavior, Prof. Primadonna's
response was, "Asking a faculty member to do 'staff work' is demeaning,
and besides, would you rather I write another article or type up minutes
that will go into the trash the next day?"

Although your institution does not treat collegiality as a separate criterion for promotion and tenure, you have become concerned that there
may be problems when Prof. Primadonna's application comes up for a
departmental vote in a few years. All these concerns are in your mind one
day when a delegation of four senior faculty members approaches you.
They are requesting you not to wait to address these issues until Prof.
Primadonna's tenure and promotion evaluation, but instead issue a letter
of non-renewal at the end of the professor's current contract.

One of your faculty members says, "If you don't do this, I don't think
I can work in this environment anymore. Either Prof. Primadonna goes,
or I'll start looking for other positions. And I know I'm not the only person who feels this way." That particular faculty member happens to be

second in productivity only to Prof. Primadonna, and you would be very
sorry to lose this person. What do you do?

Questions

1. Based on what you know so far, is the situation bad enough to war-
   rant Prof. Primadonna's non-renewal?
2. If you decide not to renew Prof. Primadonna's contract, how do you
   respond to:
   a. your dean, who is a strong supporter of Dr. Primadonna because
      of this faculty member's growing reputation as a scholar and
      increasing popularity with students?
   b. students and alumni, who demand to know why you have
      "fired" the best professor they have ever had?
   c. Prof. Primadonna, who is threatening you with a grievance
      and possible lawsuit for wrongful dismissal since collegiality
      is not one of your institution's established criteria for faculty
      evaluation?
3. If you decide that the situation does not call for an immediate non-
   renewal of Prof. Primadonna's contract:
   a. How would you mentor Prof. Primadonna so as to improve the
      situation? What advice would you give?
   b. What would you say to those members of your department who
      are threatening to leave?
   c. What would you say to the other members of your department
      who now say, "You're not looking out for *our* interests. Why
      don't you ever 'have our backs'? That's your job, after all."?
4. Imagine that you decide to renew Prof. Primadonna's contract. You
   provide guidance, and certain matters improve but the professor's
   conduct still rankles many members of the department. At the
   appropriate time, the department votes by a slender majority not
   to recommend Prof. Primadonna for tenure or promotion. Can you
   imagine any circumstances under which you would overturn the
   department's recommendation? If so, what are they?
5. The gender of Prof. Primadonna is never indicated in the case. As
   you read it, what gender did you assume Prof. Primadonna was?
   Would your reaction be any different if the professor were of the
   other gender?
6. Would your reaction be any different if Prof. Primadonna were a
   citizen of another country where it is culturally acceptable for faculty members to act this way?

7. Would the way in which you handled this situation be any different if Prof. Primadonna were a member of one of your institution's "protected classes" according to its Statement of Non-Discrimination, Statement of Inclusivity, Affirmative Action Plan, or Equal Opportunity Guidelines?

Resolution

As you reflect on the situation, you decide that if you give in to the faculty delegation and dismiss Prof. Primadonna right now, you're creating a precedent that others can use whenever they want something. ("If you don't do X, I'm going to start looking for another job.") For this reason, you make no specific promises to the faculty members who meet with you, but reassure them that you are aware of the problem and are actively taking steps to deal with it.

You tell them you fully appreciate the extent to which they are upset and that you recognize the department has a serious issue to deal with. At the same time, you remind the faculty of the appropriate mechanism they have to deal with matters of this kind: your institution's formal evaluation process. You make it clear that it will be through that process that you will address the issue.

While that process is unfolding, you decide it is a good time to have an informal mentoring session with Prof. Primadonna and discuss the specific behaviors that need to change. You feel obliged as a mentor to point out to Prof. Primadonnna the likely consequences if those changes do not occur. You reflect on whether there is a suitable member of the department (or even better, a representative of a different department that is similar to your own) who can meet regularly with Prof. Primadonna in order to provide guidance. You understand that mentors are able say things that supervisors cannot, and you conclude that Prof. Primadonna is desperately in need of someone who is not afraid to tell the truth.

Since you only have a few years before Prof. Primadonna's tenure evaluation, you decide that you will need to address the issue of collegiality in your next annual review of the professor. You conclude that Prof. Primadonna's response to that constructive criticism will be a good test. If the advice is taken in the same spirit with which it will be given—as genuinely helpful advice—you will conclude that improvement is possible. If Prof. Primadonna dismisses your advice as trivial or takes affront to your suggestions, you will regard this reaction as a hint of how much worse the problems will probably become if Prof. Primadonna is granted tenure.

CASE STUDY 2.2: DR. DULLES DISHWATER

You're a department chair at an institution that has a strong teaching mission. In fact, your school's vision statement sets a goal of becoming one of the top five teaching universities in your region within a decade. For the most part, your department is well aligned with that goal. Almost every faculty member in the program has a distinguished record in the classroom. The professors in your discipline receive excellent scores on their student evaluations, their students do well in their subsequent courses, and several of them have even won prestigious awards for their innovations in pedagogy.

That success does not apply, however, to your program's newest member, Dr. Dulles Dishwater, a first-year assistant professor with a doctorate from an Ivy League institution. Dr. Dishwater is a pleasant and very personable young man. He just does not seem to be a very good teacher, at least not yet. One day you receive a petition, signed by forty-seven students, complaining to you that Dr. Dishwater, although very nice, is a "terrible teacher." Their complaints are things you've heard before: he is disorganized; he is boring and lectures continually instead of engaging students in the material; his lessons do not relate very well to the assignments in the textbook; he frequently forgets which material he has already covered; and he has occasionally even read an entire lecture directly from his notes.

Every year your university recognizes the department with the highest overall score on student evaluations at the spring honors convocation. Although your department won this award for the past six years, this year Dr. Dishwater's scores are so low that your department does not even rank among the top five finalists. You are aware that you have a serious problem on your hands and that you need to do something about it. But what?

Questions

1. What do you do with regard to the students?
   a. Do you schedule a group meeting with all the students who signed the petition?
   b. Do you schedule a group meeting with all of Dr. Dishwater's students regardless of whether or not they signed the petition?
   c. Do you decide to schedule individual meetings with each student who signed the petition rather than meeting them in a group?
   d. Do you refuse to meet with the students at all?

  e. Do you try to find a representative sample of students in all of Dr. Dishwater's classes and meet them in focus groups?

  f. Do you do something else?

 2. What do you do with regard to Dr. Dishwater?

  a. Do you call a special meeting with Dr. Dishwater to discuss the issue?

  b. If so, do you tell him in advance the purpose of the meeting?

  c. Do you show him the petition?

  d. Do you simply address the issue during Dr. Dishwater's annual evaluation?

  e. If it is still early enough in the year to do so, do you decide not to renew Dr. Dishwater's contract for the following year?

  f. Do you assign him a mentor?

 3. What else do you do with regard to the issue?

  a. Do you act on the students' petition at all?

  b. Do you refer the matter to the dean? The provost?

  c. Do you wait and let the regular tenure and promotion evaluation process take its course in several years?

  d. Do you discuss the matter with the senior members of the department?

  e. Would you respond any differently if Dr. Dishwater were a member of a protected class?

  f. Would you respond any differently if you knew that Dr. Dishwater had spent the last year trying to cope with a contentious divorce and the care of his elderly parents at the same time that he was adjusting to being a college professor for the first time?

  g. Would you try to institute a performance plan?

Resolution

Although the students are pressing you for immediate action, you decide that it is too soon in Dr. Dishwater's service at the university for you to issue a letter of non-renewal. You choose instead to begin an extensive mentoring program with Dr. Dishwater in order to determine whether you can improve the quality of his teaching. Since you regard his positive personality and impressive education as assets to your program, you prefer to strengthen his weaknesses rather than to cut him loose on the basis of those weaknesses.

 Working closely with your institution's center for excellence in teaching and learning, you devise a detailed mentoring plan that Dr. Dishwater will be required to follow. The plan includes mandatory attendance at a certain number of pedagogical workshops each semester for three years, sitting in on the classes of several faculty members who have been designated as master teachers, and meeting regularly with a mentor who will observe Dr. Dishwater in class and coach him on how to improve.

In a meeting with the students who brought you the petition, you thank them for bringing the matter to your attention. You promise them that you will take action, but you resolutely resist their efforts to have you specify precisely what action you will take. You tell the students that personnel issues are handled privately at your university, and so you are not at liberty to reveal the exact nature of your plan. Nevertheless, you assure them that you fully support the teaching mission of the institution and are committed to taking definite action to ensure that the quality of their education will be as high as possible.

GUIDELINES FOR DEVELOPING A PERFORMANCE PLAN

Both formal and informal mentoring can lead to the development of a performance plan: a set of specific goals with deadlines by which those goals must be achieved. During informal mentoring, those goals may be regarded merely as suggestions without any implication that negative consequences will follow if the person fails to achieve them. During formal mentoring, performance plans are usually developed either as a mechanism to outline intermediate steps toward a larger goal (such as a successful application for tenure and promotion) or as a way to remediate some specific weakness (such as a significant problem identified by an evaluation process).

Regardless of whether the performance plan is formal or informal, however, there are certain guidelines to keep in mind when drawing up these plans so as to make them as effective as possible.

- *Outline specifically but humanely how the faculty member's performance needs to improve.* Saying things like "Your teaching evaluations were horrible this semester" will not produce the results you are looking for. For one thing, it comes across as a slap in the face, and the faculty member is far more likely to try to explain away or justify the low scores than to pay attention to your suggestions for improvement. For another, it does not provide the faculty member with any guidance on how to perform better. It is far preferable to say something like "I noticed that, on student course evaluations, your scores in classroom management weren't quite where we'd like them to be for the department. I'd like us to explore ways that I might be able to help you in that area. Here are a few things I'd like you to try . . ."
- *Set goals in such a way that it will be clear whether or not they are reached.* Giving a faculty member a goal like "Get those teaching evaluation

scores up" is too vague to be helpful. How much of an increase would you consider satisfactory? One hundredth of a point on a single question technically fulfills your charge, but that would not be at all sufficient if you were expecting an overall increase of at least two points per question. Be concrete in your recommendations, saying things like, "Next fall, let me see the syllabi for your courses at least a month before you need to post them. Since a lot of students are saying that your requirements aren't clear, I want to work with you in a way to phrase them so that everyone will know exactly what the assignments are."

- *Make a clear distinction between what you are requiring and what you are merely recommending.* When you mentor a faculty member who has not been meeting expectations and develop a performance plan for that person's improvement, some of the goals you set will need to be absolute requirements. In other words, if the faculty member does not fulfill that goal, certain sanctions will arise. But other recommendations you make will simply be suggestions: it would be great if the faculty member did those things but, if he or she does not, there will not be any repercussions. To the faculty member, who may well be anxious or embarrassed because you are criticizing the quality of his or her work, every suggestion can sound like a demand. Be careful to note that something is only a recommendation if that is how you regard it.

- *If a particular action is required, set a deadline.* It is easy for people to be confused about when they are expected to reach certain objectives if you do not provide them with a target date. Even if your advice is clear—such as "What we really need to have happen is for you to have at least three more research articles accepted for publication by journals that our departmental policy defines as top-tier"—that goal is still confusing since it lacks a firm deadline. Be sure to specify not only what you want done, but also when that requirement must be met.

- *If there will be repercussions for not meeting a goal, state what they will be.* Just as it is important for there to be a firm deadline in a performance plan, the faculty member must know what will happen if the specified level of performance is not reached. This requirement is particularly important in cases in which dismissal or non-renewal of a contract is a possibility. The person you are mentoring has a right to know what the stakes may be for failing to meet a goal. It helps the person make other plans in case the objective appears unattainable. Additionally, it helps prevent misunderstandings if you need to invoke a sanction.

Imagine you have been appointed as the formal mentor of the following three faculty members:

- Prof. Newby is a recently hired tenure-track assistant professor who has a lot of energy but not much experience. Both Prof. Newby's teaching evaluations and research record have been satisfactory to above average, but not stellar. In order to make Prof. Newby's promotion and tenure prospects as close to a sure thing as possible, you are asked to develop an informal, forward-looking performance plan.
- Prof. Stuck is a tenured associate professor whose research productivity declined precipitously after tenure and promotion. As a result, Prof. Stuck has become what is often called a "terminal associate professor," difficult to dismiss but with very little chance of ever becoming a full professor. As a mentor, you are asked to find a way either to jumpstart Prof. Stuck's research or to find a suitable alternative use for Prof. Stuck's talent.
- Prof. Deadwood is a tenured full professor, fifty-one years old. Prof. Deadwood receives mediocre student evaluations, attends but does not present papers at conferences, and has published only a brief op-ed piece since being promoted to full professor. Prof. Deadwood appears to be merely going through the motions until retirement, but that retirement is more than a decade away. Your task as a mentor is to reengage Prof. Deadwood into the department as a productive faculty member.

Challenge Question: How do you go about developing an effective mentoring strategy for each of these three faculty members, all of whom are at different stages of their career?

Scenario Outcome: You decide that your first step must be to determine exactly what each faculty member needs in order to improve his or her performance. You discover that Prof. Newby has a great deal of potential, but this potential has just never been tapped. Prof. Newby basically coasted through graduate school and had never been challenged to do better than just above average. Similarly you determine, after a number of very candid conversations, that Prof. Stuck is simply too temperamentally unsuited for research for promotion to full professor to be possible within the immediate future. You also discover that Prof. Stuck is a highly effective classroom teacher, so you assign Prof. Stuck as a co-mentor to help you in your effort to improve Prof. Newby's teaching.

This assignment reengages Prof. Stuck to such an extent that, within a few years, you nominate Prof. Stuck for a campus-wide teaching award. That award leads Prof. Stuck to write several articles on the scholarship of teaching, thus finally jumpstarting a return to scholarly activity. You also encourage Prof. Newby and Prof. Deadwood to meet together regularly for informal conversations. In time, Prof. Newby's energy begins to reinvigorate Prof. Deadwood, and Prof. Deadwood's long institutional history proves valuable when Prof. Newby is trying to find a way through the complex promotion and tenure process. While Prof. Deadwood never proves to be one of the department's most productive faculty members, the professor's performance does at least improve to the level of satisfactory.

You are the chair of a department with a healthy balance of faculty members at different ranks: the program is not too top-heavy with full professors, and you also do not have so many untenured assistant professors that mentoring them diverts you from other important responsibilities. The one person you are concerned about, however, is Dr. Blasé who received tenure and promotion to the rank of associate professor nine years ago. Dr. Blasé is a valuable and collegial member of your department and has had significant achievements in teaching, research, and service.

The problem is that Dr. Blasé is indifferent to the whole idea of going up for promotion to full professor. You have met with Dr. Blasé several times and gone over the steps that would be necessary for a successful application, but no action appears to have been taken. Dr. Blasé routinely claims to be "simply too busy with teaching, research, and service to devote time to the 'boring paperwork' of preparing a promotion application. My colleagues in the department know me and respect how hard I work for the discipline and our students. If that's not enough for people, I don't know what else I can say."

Challenge Questions: Is the decision to apply for promotion solely up to Dr. Blasé or do you have a professional obligation to force the issue? In either case, how do you mentor Dr. Blasé so as to promote the greatest likelihood of success and career satisfaction?

Scenario Outcome: At the vast majority of institutions, promotion to the rank of professor is somewhat different from promotion to other ranks. Most colleges and universities tie promotion to the rank of associate professor to the granting of tenure. Yet even at schools where these two processes are not linked, it is usually the practice for the two processes to occur at about the same time in a faculty member's career. For this reason, there is a strong incentive for professors to reach associate rank: if they do not, they will usually be placed on a terminal contract.

But there is no parallel incentive for people to become full professors. If faculty members reach this rank, they usually get a bit more money and prestige, but if they do not, they do not lose anything they already have. For this reason, occasionally a faculty member will choose to forego his or her final promotion. They may be afraid of failure, believe that the extra compensation simply is not worth the effort, or feel that they have better things to do with their limited time, as appears to be the case with Dr. Blasé. In this situation, you decide that, since the department already has a good balance of faculty members in various ranks, there is no compelling reason why Dr. Blasé's promotion is urgent.

You do believe, however, that for the sake of Dr. Blasé's continual development and for the example it provides the junior faculty, you should provide some gentle encouragement for Dr. Blasé to reconsider this decision periodically. You begin scheduling some informal mentoring sessions with Dr. Blasé, sometimes pointing out the benefits that come from being a full professor and describing ways in which promotions help the department, not just the faculty member. Although you experience some initial resistance, you persist in these discussions, and your ongoing support gradually begins to change Dr. Blasé's mind.

As chair you pride yourself on the close relationship you have developed with all twelve of the faculty members in your program. You are a close-knit group, frequently getting together at social events and developing friendships with one another's families. At several of these celebrations, you have noticed that one of your faculty members, Dr. Jack Daniels, seems to drink excessively. Dr. Daniels is a tenured full professor, and until this point in his career no one has regarded his drinking as a significant issue. If people noticed it at all, they dismissed it as his own business, limited to evenings and to the weekend, and causing no one any danger since Dr. Daniels does not drive: he takes a taxi everywhere he goes.

Yesterday, however, four students came to you and indicated that Dr. Daniels has recently been coming to class with alcohol on his breath. They say that his lectures are at times incoherent, and he once skipped so much material that the class did poorly on the department's standardized tests. The students say they like Dr. Daniels as a person and do not want to get him into any trouble, but they are paying a lot of money for their education and do not want their chances of getting a job after graduation hampered by, in their words, "a drunk." You assure the students that you will look into the matter and ask them not to repeat their allegations to others.

Challenge Question: How do you proceed?

Scenario Outcome: You meet with the director of human resources at your university, Mr. Jim Beam, and ask his advice. Mr. Beam explains to you the institution's Employee Assistance Program (EAP), which can provide counseling to faculty members in a number of areas, including substance abuse. After discussing the matter thoroughly, the two of you decide that Mr. Beam will have a casual conversation with Dr. Daniels, note that concerns about his drinking have been raised informally, and provide him with information about the EAP.

That solution seems appropriate to you since you are so close to Dr. Daniels that, if you raise the issue as his friend, colleague, and supervisor, you are afraid the conversation will be counterproductive: he may be so embarrassed that he will become defensive about his drinking and not seek the help he needs. Mr. Beam follows through on his suggestion and puts Dr. Daniels in touch with a licensed counselor who assesses the situation and recommends an appropriate rehabilitation clinic. Dr. Daniels's stay in the clinic is arranged to occur during the summer so that the problem is addressed discreetly with as few people as possible needing to know the details of what is occurring.

KNOW THE LIMITS OF MENTORING

Since mentors and protégés frequently develop very close relationships, the people you mentor may share some very personal information with you. Most faculty members do not compartmentalize their professional and personal lives, so your protégés may well feel that the information they are sharing with you is directly relevant to all the other issues you are discussing. When you hear about personal problems and struggles, you may be tempted to offer some advice that goes beyond your role as a department chair. Resist that urge: it comes very close to constituting practicing counseling without a license.

Advising people about their personal relationships, mental health challenges, or medical conditions is unwise—and in certain cases it may even be illegal. Leave the counseling to licensed professionals. They have the knowledge and experience necessary to determine the best course of action for problems that go beyond faculty member's academic responsibilities. Sometimes a mentor's best advice is merely "I'm afraid I just can't advise you about this issue."

CASE STUDY 2.3: MENTORING YOUR FORMER MENTOR

Most days you feel you have landed your dream job: you are a department chair at the same school you attended as an undergraduate. Almost every experience brings with it a new wave of nostalgia and, although you have at times been disillusioned to discover that your old romantic ideas about your program's "perfect faculty" do not always conform to reality, you can't imagine being as happy in any other job.

One challenge you have already had to face involved your former advisor, Dr. Chestnut. He had been a role model for you ever since you were a college freshman. He became your advisor and wrote the letter of recommendation that cleared the way for your successful admission into a prestigious graduate program. He flew more than a thousand miles to see you receive your doctoral hood, encouraged you to apply for the position you now hold in his own department, vigorously supported your application for tenure, coauthored four articles with you, and has been your strongest supporter in the program.

Once you became chair, however, you realized that Dr. Chestnut was no longer keeping up with current pedagogy in your field. Even as the university adopted a number of active learning strategies, he continued to rely on reading his lectures from aging notes. When Dr. Chestnut did depart from his lesson plans, he usually lapsed into long anecdotes that seemed to have little to do with the material of the course. The withdrawal rate from Dr. Chestnut's courses became extraordinarily high. As difficult as the conversation was, you encouraged him to retire from the faculty six years ago so that he could "devote more time to study and research." His many contributions to the discipline caused your institution to grant him emeritus status quite willingly, so that he still maintains library privileges, an office, and the right to attend department meetings.

Therein lies your new problem. Unlike other faculty with emeritus status, Dr. Chestnut now comes into the office every day and puts in hours as long as he did when he was working. But since he now has very little to do, he spends his time visiting other faculty members in their offices, distracting them from their work with long stories about what the university was like "in its heyday," and engaging them in meandering conversations when they should be preparing their courses or conducting their own research. When faculty members are not around, Dr. Chestnut stops students in the hallway for extended conversations, with the result that even majors in the department have been avoiding your corridor as much as possible.

When Dr. Chestnut comes to department meetings, he does not simply sit quietly and listen. He participates actively in every discussion and provides a great deal of advice, all of it impractical and long-winded. You hear faculty members say things like, "I thought he retired. What's he doing still around here?" Morale in the program is suffering, and the department's work on a key curriculum reform is falling behind. You go to the dean to ask for advice, and she tells you, "Well, we've never done it before, but technically we're entitled to revoke emeritus status. Is that what you want to do?"

Questions

1. Is there any way to solve the problem that also spares Dr. Chestnut's feelings?
2. What is likely to be the result if you took each of the following actions?
   a. You do nothing.
   b. You hold a department meeting with every member of the faculty except Dr. Chestnut and seek their advice.
   c. You hold a department meeting with the entire faculty present, including Dr. Chestnut, and candidly discuss what you see as the problem.
   d. You work with the dean to revoke Dr. Chestnut's emeritus status.

   e. You give Dr. Chestnut a direct order that he is not to attend any more department meetings and require him to limit his time in the office to one day a week.

   f. You move Dr. Chestnut's office to a remote location because "the department needs the space."

   g. You meet with Dr. Chestnut casually over coffee and candidly discuss the matter.

   h. You meet with Dr. Chestnut casually over coffee and ask for advice about how to handle a problem "a friend" is having with a faculty member who seems remarkably like Dr. Chestnut.

3. It is clear from this case study that Dr. Chestnut has been the most important person in your professional life. You feel loyal to him in a way that goes far beyond your feelings for any other member of the department. Is your relationship with Dr. Chestnut compromising your ability to help your department solve this problem?

Resolution

You invite Dr. Chestnut out to lunch off campus. In the course of your conversation, you express your gratitude for all he has done for you personally, particularly for serving as a great mentor. "But now," you say, "I'm afraid I need to do a little mentoring myself." You discuss your future plans for moving the department forward in new and exciting ways, building on the solid foundation he has left the program. You assure him that his legacy is safe and that you know he would not intentionally do anything to hamper the department's success.

As kindly as you can, you mention that some of the conversations with faculty members in their offices, students in the hallway, and the entire department at faculty meetings are creating difficulties for the program that you know he does not want. Other people, you continue, respect him so much that they have been hesitant to raise this issue with them. But because of the longstanding relationship the two of you share, you continue, you know he would accept this advice in the spirit with which it is offered.

When you ask him to limit the amount of time he spends in the department, it is obvious that Dr. Chestnut is simultaneously hurt by your suggestion and proud of you for having had the courage to deliver it. He concludes, "Well, it was time anyway for me to begin doing all that traveling I always said I was going to do. I guess I never would have gotten around to it if you hadn't been willing to tell me some hard truths."

CASE STUDY 2.4: AN INTIMIDATING SITUATION

You are the chair of your college's smallest department: there are only four full-time faculty members in the discipline, which means that the idiosyncrasies of any one member of the program has a far greater impact than it would in a larger department. The only full professor in your program is Dr. Fractious. You yourself are a tenured associate professor, and your other two colleagues are tenure-track assistant professors. One of your ongoing challenges as chair is that Dr. Fractious has a very strong personality and often becomes confrontational when he does not get his way.

This year, you were successful in advocating with the dean for a new faculty position. It is the first new position anyone at the institution can remember being added to your program, and the whole department is excited at the prospect of having a new colleague. Since the department is so small, all four of you serve on the search committee, which you chair. Three finalists for the position were brought to campus, interviewed, and all remain interested in the job.

Dr. Crony received a three-to-one vote on a secret ballot. You know that you were the lone dissenter because you preferred a different candidate, Dr. Stellar, whom you regarded as a much better fit for the program with a stronger record in both research and teaching. You now have to decide whether you will pass the committee's recommendation on to the dean or override it in favor of your own choice.

The college's bylaws state that the chair of the search committee must take the opinion of the full committee into account but is free to submit his or her own recommendation. While almost every search chair at the university has concurred with the committee's vote in the past, you know of at least three other cases where the chair overturned that recommendation.

You are still deciding what to do when you find an anonymous note slipped under your door. It alleges that Dr. Crony is an old friend of Dr. Fractious who had encouraged Dr. Crony to apply for the position as soon as it was posted. If true, Dr. Fractious has violated an institutional policy that requires all members of a search committee to reveal any prior relationship they have had with a candidate and to recuse themselves from any decision made about that candidate.

The note further alleges that the two untenured members of the department preferred Dr. Stellar but had been intimidated by Dr. Fractious's implication that their future at the university might be uncertain if they supported any candidate other than Dr. Crony. The note confirms your feeling that Dr. Stellar is the right candidate for the job.

Questions

1. Do you simply overrule the recommendation of the other members, pass on Dr. Stellar's application to the dean, and bear the brunt of Dr. Fractious's wrath (which you can more easily do than your colleagues because you are tenured), or do you try to address the situation first?
2. Do you speak privately with the two junior members of the department to learn whether the allegations in the anonymous note are true?
3. Do you confront Dr. Fractious about the anonymous allegation that he violated institutional policy by failing to report his prior relationship with Dr. Crony?
   a. If you do so, how do you respond if Dr. Fractious flatly denies the accusation?
   b. How do you respond if Dr. Fractious reminds you of a situation in which you yourself had failed to report your own prior relationship with a candidate during a previous search?
4. How do you mentor the two junior members of the department so that this situation does not cause them problems later when they come up for tenure?
5. How do you mentor Dr. Stellar so that Dr. Fractious's resistance to this hiring decision does not affect Dr. Stellar's morale, job satisfaction, and tenure prospects?
6. How do you mentor Dr. Fractious to avoid similar problems in the future and restore as much harmony as you can to your very small program?

Resolution

You meet with the dean over the allegations that have been made about Dr. Fractious. After further investigation, the dean and the institution's legal counsel decide that there is sufficient evidence for a formal letter of reprimand be placed in Dr. Fractious's file. The letter states that Dr. Fractious was in violation of the institutional policy requiring all search committee members to disclose any previous relationships with candidates and to recuse themselves from decisions made about those candidates. It does not mention the threats supposedly made against the two junior faculty members since you cannot support that charge without involving them.

This reprimand will bar Dr. Fractious from participating in tenure and promotion decisions regarding all junior members of the department, exclude him from receiving any merit increases for three years, and open the potential for further disciplinary action if other policies are violated in the future.

The following year you establish formal mentoring relationships with Dr. Stellar and the other two untenured faculty members in the program, working with them to set clear goals that will increase the likelihood of successful tenure and promotion evaluations, and taking steps to sustain their morale. Although it proves to be more difficult, you also reach out to Dr. Fractious, providing positive reinforcement when he exhibits good behavior, and gently advising him against any further confrontations with members of the department.

These efforts are only partially successful—several years later Dr. Fractious is the only person in the entire college who votes against your promotion to the rank of full professor—but you remain satisfied that you have made the right decision.

FOR REFLECTION

Mentoring members of the department is one of the most invisible duties most chairs have. Job descriptions frequently do not mention it, and evaluation systems often include no mechanism for rewarding it. But regardless of whether a mentoring system is formal or informal, chairs almost always end up playing this role in their programs. Since they receive their positions due to their experience in the discipline, chairs can guide faculty members who are just starting out and help them make progress both for their own sake and in the best interest of the department.

With peers and more senior colleagues, they can function as a source of advice and a sounding board for ideas. In many ways, becoming proficient as a mentor requires practice, confidentiality, and sound judgment. When chairs succeed at mentoring, their impact goes far beyond the time they devote to these tasks. They also often find it to be one of the most rewarding aspects of their jobs.

3

Promoting Teamwork and Collegiality

The way in which members of the academic community view the work of the department chair can vary dramatically. A former provost told one of this book's coauthors, "The chair sets the tone and establishes the culture for the entire department." After about a month on the job, a new chair said to the other coauthor, "I finally understand what this department chair business is all about. My job is to listen to people complain and to sign stuff." Depending on the kind of day you are having, you may agree more with the chair than the provost or vice versa. But the fact is that both perspectives contain a good deal of truth.

As chairs, we *do* end up hearing a lot of people complain and we *are* able to set the tone for our disciplines. While few of us want to turn our offices into our building's unofficial Complaint Department, many of us have seen how a toxic, uncivil, non-collegial faculty member can destroy a once-great program. So we end up listening to people complain about our colleagues, fix the problems where we can, and try to establish a more positive culture for our departments.

There are plenty of situations in which chairs can afford to adopt a wait-and-see attitude, but breaches of collegiality are not one of them. Left unchecked, incivility tends to grow. Faculty members who were previously team players begin to disengage so that they are no longer targets of abuse or ridicule. A vicious cycle follows as their example inspires others to retreat, students change majors because they find the climate in the department uncomfortable, you as chair become frustrated in your attempts to put an end to the problems, and the dean and provost become swept up in a conflict that eventually reaches their level.

When collegiality and teamwork are held in high esteem, they can become the cornerstone of the department's professional work. But when they do not exist, members of the program begin to view one another as competitors and enemies, rather than as participants in a shared effort. The department simply becomes a collection of unconnected (and frequently angry) people who happen to work in the same discipline.

WHAT COLLEGIALITY IS—AND IS NOT

The noun "collegiality" refers to cooperative interaction among colleagues. It does not suggest uniformity of thought, "political correctness," or a complete lack of dissent. It merely means that people are working with one another professionally so as to achieve the goals of the program. The adjective "collegial" is used to describe someone who, as a member of a department or program, takes an appropriate level of responsibility for the collective work of the group and interacts harmoniously so as to support the contributions of others. To put it another way, collegiality is:

- A reciprocal and cooperative relationship among colleagues.
- A commitment to sustaining a positive and productive environment.
- A type of interaction that supports all three dimensions of faculty work: teaching, research, and service.
- A collaborative approach to making decisions that relies on mutual respect.

Collegiality promotes:

- The healthy, candid, and respectful sharing of ideas.
- The freedom of all members of the group to have their own views.
- Positive and productive dissent.

Collegiality is not:

- A matter simply of "going along to get along."
- The expectation that every member of the group agree on every issue.
- A requirement that introverts become extroverts.
- A panacea for departmental discord.
- Impossible to develop in a department that is already experiencing problems with uncivil behavior.

WHAT CAN CHAIRS DO?

As a means of promoting collegiality, there are several actions that chairs can take to set the proper tone and encourage a culture of teamwork, including:

- Setting an example of collegiality. The temptation may be to respond to rude behavior with rudeness, but doing so only makes the situation worse. When faculty members are engaging in breaches of collegiality, be assertive, firm, and authoritative but polite. Other people will be taking their cue from you.
- Creating a mission statement that includes collegiality as an important component of what your program aspires to. As the hockey star Wayne Gretsky is often quoted as saying, "You miss 100% of the shots you don't take." (For Gretsky's actual words in 1984, see sportsillustrated.cnn.com/vault/article/magazine/MAG1121668/4/index.htm.) If your program does not make collegiality a goal, it may not develop spontaneously. Referring to collegiality in your mission statement keeps it in the foreground of everyone's attention, preserving it if it already exists and making it an aspiration if incivility is the norm.
- Helping faculty members understand that they are there to serve, not dictate. Being a college professor can be a heady experience: faculty members are experts in their field and are often deferred to in their subject areas. That can make them believe at times that they can dictate what everyone must do and believe, even in department meetings or a colleague's office. Mentoring your faculty members in the art of servant leadership can be an important contribution you make toward the effective interaction of everyone in the program.
- Being transparent in your own decision making. Suspicion tends to breed in environments when people believe they are not being informed about issues vital to their work. If that suspicion breeds long enough, it can erupt in hostility, aggression, and rude behavior. By adopting a transparent style of leadership, you are helping to break this cycle and promote a collegial environment for the faculty to teach and the students to learn.

For more information about the chair's role in fostering a collegial department, see Cipriano (2011), 53–71.

CASE STUDY 3.1: REAPPOINTMENT BLUES

You are a full professor who has been chairing a department of fifteen full-time faculty members for nine years. One of those fifteen faculty members, Dr. Noxious, is an untenured assistant professor in her third year at the university. Her colleagues have informed you privately that Dr. Noxious is frequently unwilling to collaborate on projects and does not take constructive criticism well. Last semester you witnessed several incidents that caused you serious concern. On two separate occasions, you heard her use language while criticizing students that you regarded as unnecessarily harsh and hurtful.

Another time, when a student challenged a grade that Dr. Noxious had given, she dismissed him abruptly and, in your opinion, rather unprofessionally. Other students observed the latter incident, and about a dozen of them then dropped the course. Her student course evaluations are very inconsistent: some students find her brash style refreshing; others feel demeaned and disrespected by her attitude. In faculty meetings, you have heard how biting her remarks can be when she believes someone has not fully considered a proposal or is wasting her time. The administrative assistant in the department avoids Dr. Noxious whenever possible since she is very condescending to the staff.

In last year's annual evaluation, you recommended that Dr. Noxious be reappointed with reservations. That rating is the second-lowest score you can give to tenure-track faculty members, since the scale runs: (1) Recommend enthusiastically; (2) Recommend; (3) Recommend with reservations; or (4) Do not recommend. In the comments section of the written evaluation, you noted concerns that other members of the program regard Dr. Noxious as a poor colleague and that you have personally witnessed her disrespectful behavior toward students, colleagues, and members of professional staff. You recommended that Dr. Noxious find a mentor who can work with her to help prevent her interpersonal style from causing her professional problems in the future. You have no reason to believe that Dr. Noxious took this advice or that her behavior has improved. Now it is time to write this year's evaluation, and you need to decide which of the four ratings to give her in regard to renewal of her contract. What do you do?

Questions

1. Is this a collegiality issue, or are Dr. Noxious's actions protected as free speech?

2. Is this a teamwork issue, or is Dr. Noxious entitled to her own personality?
3. What is likely to be the result if you took each of the following actions?
   a. You refer the matter to the dean.
   b. You ask each faculty member for his or her opinion.
   c. You recommend that Dr. Noxious not be reappointed.
   d. You recommend that Dr. Noxious be reappointed and make additional suggestions as to how her performance needs to improve.
   e. You seek the advice of other chairs at your university.
   f. You seek the advice of the Office of Human Resources.
4. Would your decision be different if any of the following were true?
   a. If Dr. Noxious were a man instead of a woman.
   b. If Dr. Noxious were a member of a seriously underrepresented group that your institution regards as a protected class.
   c. If you thought you would lose this position if you did not renew Dr. Noxious's contract.
   d. If Dr. Noxious were far more popular with the students than is described in the case study.
   e. If Dr. Noxious were an internationally renowned researcher and your department's leading recipient of grants.
   f. If Dr. Noxious had a record of being litigious and making the life of anyone who crossed her miserable.
   g. If Dr. Noxious were a close friend of the provost.
   h. If Dr. Noxious were married to the provost.

Resolution

You decide that there are several key factors at work here. First, you do not know for sure whether Dr. Noxious took your advice about working with a mentor (although you *believe* she did not) and that several incidents involving Dr. Noxious were simply the result of her aggressive, very forceful personality. Second, although her comments to students were ill-advised since they caused a number of students to drop the course, you only witnessed exchanges that, *in your opinion*, were unnecessarily harsh, hurtful, and unprofessional; she did not technically violate any institutional policies. Third, regardless of whether Dr. Noxious met with a mentor or not, you have not seen any improvement in her collegiality, and you have no reason to believe that her behavior will improve if she eventually receives tenure. Fourth, while Dr. Noxious has a right to be her own person, her behavior is causing problems for the department in terms of excessive student withdrawals and the unwillingness of the faculty and staff to work with her.

One faculty member in your department, Dr. Amiable, has been acting quite subdued for the last week. In the past she was outgoing, pleasant, and always optimistic. In fact, you have long regarded Dr. Amiable as the very essence of collegiality. Prior to the start of today's department meeting, however, Dr. Amiable did not acknowledge any of her colleagues in the department. During discussion of the first item on the agenda, she suddenly became curt and made an insulting remark to another faculty member. You ignored her action the first time since it was so out of character, but throughout the meeting she becomes increasingly hostile to her colleagues and angrily dismisses any of their attempts to calm her down.

Challenge Question: Do you intervene at the meeting and openly address Dr. Amiable's behavior in front of her colleagues?

Scenario Outcome: You decide to adjourn the meeting because it is becoming unproductive. You then ask Dr. Amiable to meet with you privately and, when you're alone, mention your concerns. "You didn't seem to be yourself in the meeting just now," you say, "and your comments to other people were causing them to shut down. We weren't really getting anything accomplished. I'm concerned about you." You try to demonstrate that you genuinely care about Dr. Amiable as a valued colleague and want to assist with any professional difficulties she might be having.

After some coaxing, she notes that everything seems to be going wrong for her at once: a major grant proposal she had worked very hard on was not funded, her children have been bullied in school, and her graduate assistant just announced that he was dropping out of the program. She says she feels that no one is supporting her: Her colleagues are too busy with their own projects to help with her grant proposal, the principal at her children's school seems more interested in the bully's rights than her children's, and she's taking her graduate assistant's departure personally.

You assure her that you will get her all the help she needs in revising and resubmitting her grant proposal, give her the phone number of someone on the school board who can help her with the bullying issue, and suggest that she take the rest of the day off. As her colleagues come in one by one to check on what happened, you preserve Dr. Amiable's confidentiality but suggest that they all "cut her some slack" for the next week or so. You also decide that it might be time for a social event in the department to help people build stronger bonds outside the workplace.

You are the chair of a small but dynamic department that has about thirty students in its graduate program, none of whom are full-time students because they all hold full-time jobs. For this reason, scheduling your department's courses at times when students can enroll is an ongoing challenge. One of the courses required for the program has regularly been taught on Tuesdays from 8:00 until 10:30 p.m. In accordance with the standards of your accrediting body, only two of your faculty members, Dr. Immovable and Dr. Inflexible, have the appropriate credentials to teach this course.

One day, they both appear in your office and announce that, because of their research commitments, neither of them wants to teach an evening class next year. You explain the need for scheduling the course at a time when it does not conflict with other classes and when the students in the program can take it. Moreover, you show them the results of a student survey you conducted last year.

Overwhelmingly, the graduate students prefer evening courses that run from 5:00 until 7:30 and from 8:00 until 10:30 so that they can keep their jobs, take classes only one or two nights a week, and still graduate in a timely manner. Neither Dr. Immovable nor Dr. Inflexible seems to care. They both still want their schedules to serve their own needs, not the needs of the students.

Challenge Question: How do you deal with this problem?

Scenario Outcome: You call a special meeting of the department to address the issue. You present the results of the student survey and argue that, if the program does not offer a schedule that meets the needs of the students, enrollment will suffer and faculty positions will be lost. Gradually the other faculty members begin to urge Dr. Immovable and Dr. Inflexible to be more accommodating.

A consensus arises that there will be a rotating schedule of graduate courses offered at the times students say they want them. With this schedule, everyone will teach one course in the 8:00 to 10:30 p.m. slot every other year. For the sake of ésprit de corps, you volunteer to teach one of these courses next semester. That will allow Dr. Immovable or Dr. Inflexible to teach the required course from 5:00 to 7:30 p.m. for one year instead. You let them decide between themselves which of them will teach in the early evening next year while the other resumes the late evening class the following year. You also agree to look into the possibility of freeing any faculty member who teaches during the 8:00 to 10:30 p.m. period from any undergraduate courses in the morning that semester. While the plan is far from perfect, most people agree it is reasonable and fair.

Since you still have several years before making a tenure decision, you decide that another recommendation with reservations is warranted. It will provide you with the paper trail you need in case you decide to recommend against tenure in the next few years, and gives you an opportunity to offer additional advice to help her improve. You begin keeping careful notes (which, as you now realize, you should have been keeping all along) on Dr. Noxious's interactions with others and make sure the dean is aware of the situation. With the dean's support, you enlist the help of key people at the university, including such offices as human resources, legal counsel, the faculty union (if applicable), and the state's attorney general (if applicable).

You now no longer recommend that Dr. Noxious work with a mentor; you require it, and you say that you will need regular reports that these meetings are occurring and that progress is being made in order to avoid a recommendation for non-renewal next year. In your evaluation you take care to focus on the specific behaviors that Dr. Noxious must change. You avoid any references to her personality or points of view. You resolve to review the case history that documents how consistently U.S. courts have affirmed an institution's use of collegiality as a factor regarding faculty employment, tenure, and termination, even if collegiality is never mentioned as a requirement in the faculty handbook or policy manual.

HOW SHOULD CHAIRS HANDLE BREACHES OF COLLEGIALITY?

The coauthors surveyed 351 academic leaders and presented them with the following scenario.

You are a tenured associate professor who, for the last seven years, has served as the chair of a department containing nine full-time faculty members. One member of your department, Dr. Ghastly, is a tenured full professor who is consistently sarcastic, degrading, and demeaning to students and faculty alike. You have spoken to him about your concerns on many occasions, and he has replied that he has academic freedom to speak his mind as he sees fit. You also wrote him a letter concerning his behavior; he never responded. You wanted to meet with him to discuss the situation, and he refused. In desperation, you speak twice with your dean who tells you that you may only use one of the following three approaches in addressing the situation. Which do you choose?

Option 1: Just leave him alone. Do nothing. Maybe he'll retire soon. It's not worth the aggravation to try to fix an unfixable situation.

Option 2: Shower him with praise. Do everything you can to win him over. Assume that his bad attitude is a result of how he feels he's being treated. Give him the courses and teaching schedule he wants. Support him in every way possible.

Option 3: Do everything you can to make his life as miserable as possible. Give him a five-day-a-week teaching schedule with classes at the most inconvenient times. Refuse to give him summer employment. Deny him travel money. Reassign him the worst office in the least desirable location the school has available.

The respondents preferred Option 2 (42.8 percent), followed by Option 1 (35.7 percent), and then by Option 3 (21.4 percent). The academic leaders were then asked two follow-up questions: (1) Have you ever been the supervisor of a faculty member who reminds you (at least to some extent) of Dr. Ghastly? (57.1 percent said they had), and (2) If you were not limited to the dean's three options, what would you do? As might be expected, when respondents were given a chance to determine their own solution to the problem, their answers were quite varied. Some wanted to terminate Dr. Ghastly immediately. Others wanted to create a detailed performance plan. Still others wanted to handle the situation more informally, viewing the problem as a "teachable moment."

But here's the interesting part: *None of the respondents who said they had experienced an incident like the one described in the scenario chose the dean's Option 3.* Not one. In other words, people who had actually had an encounter with a toxic, non-collegial faculty member were *least* likely to be attracted by the possibility of a punitive response. To some readers, that result may seem counterintuitive. We might think that the more exposed we are to toxic, unprofessional behavior, the more likely we would be to want to punish those who are guilty of such behavior. But the opposite is the case.

As chairs become more experienced and learn from their own dealings with uncivil members of the faculty, they discover that taking retribution on those who violate departmental collegiality simply does not work. In many cases, retaliation even backfires: it makes the faculty member whose behavior is poor act even worse and sets an example for others that punitive actions are the appropriate response to incivility. Positive leadership strategies such as reinforcing good behavior, engaging in non-confrontational discussions about problems, and promoting teamwork tend to be far more successful.

CASE STUDY 3.2: THE LOOSE CANNON

You are a full professor in a midsized department of sixteen full-time faculty members and eleven adjuncts. Your colleagues and the dean recently gave you their unanimous support to serve as the department's chair after the previous chair retired. Dr. Lou Scannon, an untenured assistant professor in your department, is about to be considered for tenure and promotion to the rank of associate professor. Dr. Scannon is better than average as a teacher and meets your program's standards for promotion in terms of research.

The problem is that Dr. Scannon is not a good team player. The former chair complained to you on several occasions that Dr. Scannon went over her head to the dean on several issues. You are also aware that he has a habit of not showing up for meetings of committees to which he is appointed, but when that committee makes a recommendation to the full department, Dr. Scannon feels free to undermine that recommendation if he does not agree with it. Several members of the department have spoken individually with Dr. Scannon about these issues. Although he always promises to act differently, his behavior never changes.

Your department weights teaching at 50 percent of the tenure and promotion decision, research at 45 percent, and service at only 5 percent. So even if Dr. Scannon is rated unsatisfactory in service, he still meets your program's requirements in 95 percent of the criteria for promotion and tenure. Complicating your decision further, your institution is undergoing an extended period of budget problems. For the last four years, no one who has had a terminal contract after a negative tenure decision has been replaced, and you are not at all confident that any new full-time faculty positions will be granted in your department if you let Dr. Scannon go. You must make a recommendation regarding his tenure application very soon.

Questions

1. Do you recommend for or against the tenure and promotion of Dr. Lou Scannon?

2. If you recommend Dr. Scannon for promotion and tenure, how important are each of the following factors in your decision?
   a. The likelihood that you will lose the position if Dr. Scannon is not tenured.
   b. The very small amount of weight assigned to service in your program.
   c. The fact that, although Dr. Scannon's behavior is far from perfect, he is not overtly hostile or rude to other members of the department.
   d. Your feeling that, with good mentoring, Dr. Scannon's problems can be solved.
3. If you recommend against his promotion and tenure, how important are each of the following factors in your decision?
   a. Dr. Scannon's history of going over the chair's head to the dean.
   b. Dr. Scannon's failure to attend committee meetings.
   c. Dr. Scannon's habit of undermining his colleagues at department meetings.
   d. Dr. Scannon's record of satisfactory to good teaching and research but lack of genuine excellence in these areas.
   e. Your own "gut feelings."
4. If your department does not require it, do you canvas the rest of the faculty for their thoughts on this issue?
5. Would your decision be any different if:
   a. Several members of the department told you that, in recent months, Dr. Scannon has become much more of a team player, begun attending committee meetings, and volunteered for several new service assignments?
   b. Dr. Scannon had an application under review for a multimillion dollar grant that was likely to be funded next year?
   c. Dr. Scannon were a scholar from another country where there is no tradition of professors performing service roles in their departments?
   d. Dr. Scannon occupied a line that was funded from outside the department and that did not exist until he was hired?
   e. Dr. Scannon were married to the president of the institution?

Resolution

You decide that, although you can make a case for Dr. Scannon's tenure and promotion, you cannot make a *strong* case. His teaching was described as *above average*, not excellent. His research was described as *meeting the standards of the department*, not surpassing them. Even though service counts as a very small percentage in the overall evaluation, Dr.

Scannon's behavior has affected more than just the service of the department. His reluctance to do committee work and willingness to undermine you and the other members of the department also has an impact on your area's teaching and research.

In your view, a tenure decision is not just about the individual; it is also about the degree to which a person fits within the program's overall needs. Even if Dr. Scannon's behavior has improved recently, that change may simply be a *tenure surge* (the extra effort that some faculty members exert shortly before a tenure decision is due). Your instincts tell you that Dr. Scannon will not be a good colleague for the long term, and you decide to trust your instincts.

You meet with the dean to make your case for being able to replace Dr. Scannon after his contract is not renewed. You point out the fact that you have had to hire eleven adjuncts just to meet the courses you currently offer to your students. That problem will only get worse without a replacement for Dr. Scannon. In a professional manner, you explain that you have made a tough call with the best interests of the institution in mind by not tenuring someone who has failed to become a team player.

You ask the dean to make a tough call in return by letting your program keep this much-needed position. If the dean responds favorably to your argument, let her know how much you appreciate this difficult decision. If your dean's decision is not to replace Dr. Scannon, thank her for her time and ask her to reconsider your request as soon as finances improve. The decision to award tenure to a faculty member who is a bad fit for your program should not be dictated by the threat of losing the position. In the long run, you would probably suffer more by having Dr. Scannon on the faculty than by losing the position.

CASE STUDY 3.3: HIRING A NEW DEAN

You are one of the department chairs who serves on the search committee for a new dean of your college. The former dean had a long, successful, and enduring relationship with the university: she was a student, faculty member, and chair before being selected as dean. But that stability has come with a cost. You have long believed that the college was being held back because it was not exposed enough to new ideas. For this reason, you view the current search as critical. The college has an opportunity to reinvent itself and to become much more prominent than it was in the past.

Complicating this situation, however, is the institution's ongoing budget crisis. There have been no raises for five years. Building maintenance has been deferred. Only critical equipment has been replaced.

Many faculty members are using computers that are now badly out of date, and you believe research and teaching have suffered as a result. The best thing about the college is its good collegial spirit. People genuinely get along with their peers. Morale is good, and the last thing you would want to do is to destroy the positive team spirit that has developed.

Therein lies your dilemma. Despite your desire to move the college forward, most of the faculty members you talk to want a dean who will not implement significant changes. You frequently hear sentiments like, "We don't need someone who comes in here and rocks the boat," "What we've got right now is working. Let's not throw the baby out with the bathwater," and "If it ain't broke, don't fix it." Even in your own department, most people seem content with the status quo. As a result, you feel torn between your own desire for the college to start moving in a bold new direction and your responsibility to reflect the concerns of the faculty.

In the best of all worlds, you would select a dean who is a resilient, articulate, and persuasive team builder, someone who has fresh ideas coupled with the diplomacy needed to put those ideas into effect. Unfortunately, even though there were more than 200 applicants for this position, none of them had this perfect profile. Along with the other members of the search committee, you have selected three finalists:

- Dr. Stillwater has been described by his references as "congenial, pleasant to work with, and always calm in a crisis, but not an idea person." During his interviews, you concluded that Dr. Stillwater will never help the college improve its reputation or develop the quality of teaching and scholarship that is needed. He has limited publications and has received only a few small grants. Dr. Stillwater served as associate dean for the past four years at one of your peer institutions and holds a doctorate degree from a mid-level state university.
- Dr. Brash is a prolific researcher with many highly regarded referred journal articles to her credit. Even in her interviews, she shared what you regarded as some innovative ideas about the future of the college. What concerns you, however, is how fixed she seemed in all her opinions. If someone started to present a different perspective, she would interrupt and reiterate her own views. Her references, while generally positive, included terms like "high maintenance," "assertive," and "obstinate." A colleague at Dr. Brash's school told you that, after going through the motions of consulting many key stakeholders about a recent policy decision, she went ahead and did exactly what everyone thought she would do all along. Dr. Brash

has been acting dean of her college for the past two years during a difficult search for the permanent dean and holds a doctorate from a prestigious private university.

- Dr. Darkhorse has had a more unusual career path. She spent several years after graduate school running her own company and then left the workforce for eight years to start a family. When she returned to work, she began as an adjunct instructor but rose quickly through the ranks until she became a department chair and coordinator of her college's faculty development effort. Although she has never been a dean or even an associate dean, many people on the search committee felt that her personal and professional experience gave her a broader perspective than most other candidates. In her interviews, she said all the right things—discussing the importance of building a team and seeking consensus—but she could provide very few examples of actually having done that. Her doctorate is from a flagship state university.

The search committee is about to meet and recommend one of these three candidates. Given your parallel desires to move the college forward, which one do you intend to support?

Questions

1. Each candidate holds a doctorate from a different kind of school: a mid-level state university, a prestigious private university, and a flagship state university. To what extent does that difference affect your decision?
2. Is there any value in getting the perspective of the former dean before you make up your mind?
3. Would your recommendation change if any collection of the following were true?
   a. You get a recommendation from the faculty in your department that ranks Dr. Stillwater first, Dr. Darkhorse second, and Dr. Brash third.
   b. You discover that a straw poll of all the faculty in the college ranks Dr. Darkhorse first, Dr. Brash second, and Dr. Stillwater third.
   c. Dr. Brash is a member of a protected class according to your institution's anti-discrimination policy.
   d. The institution where Dr. Darkhorse had her rapid rise is your own. She is now one of your colleagues as department chair.
   e. Your position as chair is very tenuous. You already know that a significant portion of the department wants you to step down,

and you sense that resistance will grow if people learn that you did not advocate on behalf of their recommendation.

f. Prior to the search, the provost told you, "I'm putting you on the search committee because I agree with you that things need to be shaken up in your college. Don't worry if others disagree with you: I've got your back."

Resolution

Even though you went into this search with a desire to bring about change in your college, you decide that the candidate who has the best chance of accomplishing that goal, Dr. Brash, has too many liabilities. Her stubbornness, even during the interview, does not bode well for the future, particularly for a college that has already established a relatively high level of teamwork. Dr. Stillwater certainly seems likely to preserve that congenial atmosphere but at the cost of continued stagnation, possibly even decline. You decide to take a chance on Dr. Darkhorse. Her unusual background may well introduce the new ideas into your college that you are hoping for, and she seems at least responsive to (if not particularly experienced in) the importance of promoting collegiality and teamwork.

At first the other members of the search committee are surprised by your choice, but they are gradually persuaded by your reasons and begin to see the problems with the other two candidates. Your committee recommends Dr. Darkhorse to the provost who, as it turns out, preferred Dr. Brash all along. There is a difficult meeting in which you find yourself compelled to serve as the primary advocate for Dr. Darkhorse's candidacy. The provost does not agree but finally gives in when faced with a unanimous recommendation of the search committee. "Okay, I'm counting on you now to make this work," the provost tells you, "since Dr. Darkhorse came with your recommendation. Work with her to see if you can get some progress under way in the college. I respect your opinion but I still have doubts about this recommendation."

PROMOTING TEAMWORK

A team may be defined as a group of people who have a high degree of interdependence and work collaboratively toward the achievement of a goal or the completion of a task. A team adopts more of a group identity than can be found in other collections of individuals, such as a committee, crowd, or gathering. Departments become teams when the faculty and staff in the program begin to see part of their identity as being a member of the Department of XYZ. They thus become much more likely to put the good of the department ahead of narrow self-interest and to make sacrifices on behalf of their colleagues. Teams are effective work groups because they develop a synergy that produces energy and creativity far beyond their capacity as individuals.

While a department chair cannot turn a department into a team on his or her own, the chair's commitment to teamwork is an absolute prerequisite for this high level of motivation, coordination, and cooperation to occur. One way of advancing this goal is to help the members of the program become more intentional about how they interact with other people on the team. For example, you might conduct a group exercise during a retreat or faculty meeting in which people work first independently and then collectively in identifying those qualities that best reflect the spirit of teamwork in the department. The product that results is less important than the process that created it. The very act of sharing ideas, making compromises, dealing with differences, and coming together in agreement helps meld the individuals of a program into a team. As a sample of what a department might produce, here is a model of the sort of statement your faculty and staff could create.

The Qualities of Teamwork in the Department of XYZ

As a department, we believe that we work together as much more than a mere collection of individuals. The strength of the Department of XYZ may be found in five qualities that help define who we are:

1. *Inclusiveness.* When we speak of the "members of the department," we do not speak of the faculty alone. Membership in the Department of XYZ is highly inclusive and extends to graduate students, those on the professional staff, undergraduate majors, non-majors who enroll in our courses, and supporters in the community, as well as both full-time and adjunct members of the faculty.
2. *Unity.* Despite our differences as individuals, members of the Department of XYZ are unified in their dedication to high academic standards, integrity, transparency, collegiality, professionalism, and tolerance.
3. *Collaboration.* We recognize that all members of our team are dependent on one another. We accept that the department working together is stronger than anyone acting alone. We strive to work together in a spirit of collaboration so as to achieve the goals of our program as a whole.
4. *Communication.* The Department of XYZ believes that unproductive conflict often results from poor communication. To avoid this

You are the chair of the smallest department at your institution: there are only three full-time faculty members. You have served as chair for twelve years and prided yourself on building a close-knit team from the faculty and staff. That is why it surprises you to learn that one member of your department, Dr. Jekyll, has been reported as speaking very critically about you behind your back. It is not the criticism itself that you mind, but the caustic and hurtful language Dr. Jekyll is said to have used, as well as the fact that he never mentioned any of these concerns to you himself.

In fact, Dr. Jekyll is always quite pleasant to you and, when you asked him whether he had any objections to what you were doing or any issues he wanted to discuss with you, he seemed surprised by the question and said no. Then, not even a week later, two other faculty members at the university reported that at a party the night before, Dr. Jekyll was quite vocal in complaining about you and said that you are "ruining the program."

Challenge Question: How do you respond to this new information?

Scenario Outcome: Teamwork is critical in any unit, but in such a small department, its importance becomes even greater. You decide that either Dr. Jekyll is trying to undermine you or someone else is spreading false rumors to undermine both of you. After hearing similar stories from several different witnesses, you decide that Dr. Jekyll has been two-faced in his denials to you and that he really has been complaining about you behind your back.

You decide to meet with Dr. Jekyll in a casual setting off campus, make it clear that a number of people are reporting to you what he has said, and clear the air. In doing so, you see a new and far angrier side of Dr. Jekyll than you had ever known existed. He spends more than an hour venting to you about his frustrations and focuses most of his anger on you personally. Rather than becoming defensive at these accusations, you decide the best strategy is to help repair the teamwork that had been one of your department's greatest strengths.

You make it clear to Dr. Jekyll that you are listening to his concerns, resolve to make a few changes that actually seem to you to be good suggestions, and reiterate that he can always come to you to discuss any concerns that he may have. You try to end the conversation on an upbeat note, reminding Dr. Jekyll how much you value your two colleagues in the program and hope you can count on his support.

problem, we commit ourselves to interact candidly with one another while always being aware of the need to distinguish between opinions and the people who hold those opinions.

5. *Identification.* We all identify with one another as members of the Department of XYZ. Our emails and letters all include this identification, and we announce our name and department whenever we answer the telephone. We hold ourselves and others to these high standards and try, whenever possible, to shift our thinking from "I" to "we."

The list of qualities developed by your department will certainly be different, reflecting the unique nature of your program and the people within it. But if people in your discipline are having difficulty completing this exercise, you might distribute the sample above as a starting point to determine what they agree and disagree with.

FOR REFLECTION

Although we have seen that no chair can create a team spirit alone, there are several tools you have in your toolkit that can lay the groundwork for transforming your program into a team:

1. Use department meetings to discuss shared goals and objectives frequently. Don't let your meetings get bogged down in the minutiae of day-to-day business.
2. Make it clear that you see the department as an environment in which all opinions will be heard, considered, and respected.
3. Share leadership tasks. Empower others by assigning them both responsibility and authority. Don't try to rule the department by decree.
4. Work with others to develop policies on how you would handle conflicts and other challenges *before* they occur.
5. Go out of your way to include people in discussions who may be intimidated by other members of the program. Ask them to state their opinions openly and thank them for their candor.
6. Try to maintain a healthy balance between the goals of the team as a whole and the goals of each member of the team. Remember that, despite what the organizational chart may say, no faculty member actually "works for" you. They all have private dreams that you can help make a reality if you choose.

4

Communicating Effectively

We may not often think of communication when listing the skills that department chairs need to develop, but effective communication is vital to nearly every aspect of the chair's position. Part of its importance results from the chair's position within the institutional hierarchy. Chairs are responsible for both communicating the decisions of the dean and upper administration to the faculty and communicating the perspectives of the faculty to the dean and upper administration. Chairs also have to be effective when they communicate with one another since departments rely on each other for service courses, electives for their students, and a united front when there is a difference of opinion between departmental leaders and the dean or provost.

In addition, the chair's role in setting the tone for his or her department is accomplished through daily informal communication with faculty, staff, and students. For this reason, good communication skills are among the most important tools chairs have in their toolkits, and the time they invest in improving their ability to communicate effectively is amply rewarded in the success of their programs.

There are many barriers to communicating effectively, among which we find:

1. *Information overload.* Faculty members are often so overwhelmed with their teaching, scholarship, committee work, emails, and other demands on their time that they may sometimes fail to communicate in a productive and timely manner.

2. *Status differences.* Although we may regard the university as a place where everyone is on an equal footing, differences in status or power affect much of what we do: graduate students often regard themselves as holding a more important position than undergraduates, faculty may feel that way about the staff, associate professors about assistant professors, deans about chairs, and so on. Those status differences often form a barrier to effective communication when people either edit themselves because they believe their voices will not be heard by those in a higher position, or shut down those who occupy a lower rank because they regard their views as unimportant.

3. *Past history.* We all bring baggage with us, and that baggage affects how we communicate with others. One particularly poor experience with a boss may make us feel that all supervisors are untrustworthy. Certain words can serve as triggers for negative emotions. Someone who once did us a favor may cloud our judgment about his or her less positive behavior. No matter who we are and what position we hold, our past interpersonal relationships play a significant role.

4. *Workload.* Just as information often overwhelms people, so do the expectations placed on members of the faculty, staff, and administration. A response might be interpreted as brusque or rude when it was actually all the person had time for in the midst of numerous pressing responsibilities. We might become frustrated when someone does not respond to our "quick question," unaware that quick questions may often have far longer and more complex answers that the other person simply has not yet had time to provide.

5. *Cultural diversity.* One of the great strengths of higher education is the way in which it exposes every member of the community to those who are very different from them in appearance, beliefs, and background. But those very differences may be impediments to communication. We may misinterpret body language, phrasing, and gestures that mean different things in different cultures.

6. *Cultural changes.* The widespread use of social media has made many people comfortable sharing intimate details of their lives that previous generations would have considered extremely private. People have different expectations for the tone, grammar, and punctuation used in professional communications versus commonly accepted standards in texts, emails, and online postings. If the recipient of a communication is anticipating that someone will adhere to these professional standards, while the person doing the communication views it as merely a private exchange, miscommunication can result.

CASE STUDY 4.1: DIDN'T SEE IT COMING

The Department of Congeniality is one of eight units within the College of Euphoria at Bliss University. As chair you have prided yourself on maintaining good relationships with your fellow chairs—all except for one: Dr. Precipitous Blindsider. Dr. Blindsider has an annoying habit of finding some problem in your department and then asking you about it in a very public manner. While these uncomfortable moments do occur occasionally with other chairs, you seem to be on the receiving end of most of them. It would not bother you very much if Dr. Blindsider was merely being annoying, but she seems to have the dean's ear. She was formerly a faculty member in his department, and the two of them are like-minded about most issues.

In your last encounter of this type, Dr. Blindsider accused you in front of the dean of adopting new policies that were disadvantageous to her students. "I do have one question today," Dr. Blindsider began at the regular roundtable discussion that ends every meeting of the dean and the chairs. "Why has the Department of Congeniality put such low enrollment caps on its service courses? That policy continually creates hardships for my students. Everyone who's majoring in my area has to take Principles of Sociability 201, a requirement that we adopted, frankly, just to help out that department with its traditionally low enrollments.

"And I think everyone here today knows what I mean. Anyway, now that we've submitted our new curriculum to our accrediting body, we're stuck with that course requirement for the next ten years. But the Department of Congeniality only runs ten sections of that course each year, capping those sections at twenty-five students each.

"Students in my department are sick and tired of being closed out of a course they have to take and, without it, can't graduate. We've got a backlog of maybe 300, 400 students who are stuck now because they can't get into this one course. Well, I did some checking and found that this course is taught at the University of Minimal Standards with 75 to 100 students per section, at Rival State University with caps of 50, and at Substandard Regional College with sections of 65.

"I've tried repeatedly to get this issue resolved, and now I need to know"— at this point Dr. Blindsider looks directly at you—"what are you going to do about the problem you've caused?"

You're caught off-guard because, despite Dr. Blindsider's claim that she has "tried repeatedly to get this issue resolved," no one has ever mentioned the "problem" to you until now. You strongly doubt the claim that 300 or 400 students have been closed out of the course, but since you did not know that the subject was going to come up at today's meeting, you did not bring any data to refute it.

You start to defend yourself by pointing out that it is very misleading to compare your course to that which is offered at other universities because your syllabus is writing-intensive, has a lab component (with labs that are limited to only twenty-five students for safety reasons), and sets far more rigorous standards. In addition, you have been asking Dr. Blindsider for several years to give you an estimate of the number of seats she needs a semester or two in advance, but you never get a response.

"Besides," you continue "if you look at the larger trends . . ." But you get no further in your defense. You notice that Dr. Blindsider and the dean are rolling their eyes at one another. You turn toward the other chairs for support and notice that they are all looking uncomfortably at the floor and pretending to be busy with handouts the dean has distributed. What do you do now?

Questions

1. What is the best strategy to take immediately when you observe Dr. Blindsider and the dean rolling their eyes?
2. What is the best strategy to adopt with Dr. Blindsider after the meeting?
3. What is the best strategy to adopt with the dean after the meeting?
4. Can your fellow chairs be of any help to you, or would trying to enlist their help cause more damage than it is worth?
5. What might occur if you tried to beat Dr. Blindsider at her own game by making announcements of this sort at future meetings?
6. Would your decision be different if:
   a. Dr. Blindsider were not friendly with the dean?
   b. You were in your last year as chair and had already decided you would return to the faculty next year?
   c. You aspired to be a dean in the not too distant future?
   d. As a faculty member, Dr. Blindsider had been president of a strong faculty union?
   e. Dr. Blindsider were the provost's wife?
   f. Dr. Blindsider was scheduled to retire at the end of the current year?

Resolution

Although this problem was created publicly, you decide that it is best resolved privately. Given the collusion that appears to be occurring between Dr. Blindsider and the dean, you wait until after the meeting, invite Dr. Blindsider out for coffee off campus, and then voice your concerns. You tell her that her behavior in the meeting was not appropriate and that you are not going to tolerate it again. You give other examples in which she has ambushed you and your fellow chairs at meetings and note that you do not expect such behavior from a colleague.

Afterward, you also meet with the dean and say you were disappointed you were not given any support during Dr. Blindsider's very personal attack on you and your department. With data now in hand, you present your side of the story and point out that important issues tend to get overlooked when Dr. Blindsider acts in this way at public meetings.

Now that you are aware of Dr. Blindsider's communication style, you resolve to confront her immediately if she ever launches a public attack against you again. For example, you decide that what you should have said at the meeting when the attack happened was, "Look, you may claim that you've tried repeatedly to get this issue resolved, but you know as well as I do that this is the very first time you've ever mentioned it to me. And I don't appreciate the way you've done it. So rather than wasting everyone's time, let's get some real numbers and see if your claim of a 300- to 400-student backlog is accurate. If it's not—well, I'm sure your apology will be just as public as your accusations."

CASE STUDY 4.2: THE PASSIVE-AGGRESSIVE FACULTY MEMBER

You are the chair of a small but vibrant department consisting of more than 200 undergraduate students but only four full-time faculty members. One faculty member, Dr. Will Knott Doitt, is a good teacher who is generally liked by the students and other faculty members, but he is unproductive in other areas. He produced enough research to receive tenure and become an associate professor, but then gradually stopped publishing. He does not write grants, make presentations at conferences, or aspire to become a full professor. In fact, he has not even *attended* a conference in more than a decade.

You have tried mentoring Dr. Doitt but find it very frustrating to communicate with him. He has a pleasant demeanor and always agrees to do whatever you ask, but then he never actually does so. Dr. Doitt is never abusive, abrasive, or disrespectful to students, faculty, or staff. He never raises his voice or offends people. The most common comment on his student course evaluations is that he is "a nice guy." One day, the three full-time faculty members of the department request a meeting with you to discuss their own concerns about Dr. Doitt. As the meeting progresses, you become aware that Dr. Doitt's behavior has had a negative effect on their workload.

1. Dr. Doitt never gets around to advising any students. If you and the four other faculty members split the advising load equally, you'd each have about forty advisees. But the other faculty members point out that the average advising load at the university is nineteen students. Since Dr. Doitt does not assume his fair share (or any share for that matter), each of you now has fifty students to advise each semester. Moreover, that total does not include meeting with new students who may wish to transfer into your department. Even worse, because of the number of meetings you have to attend, the other members of the department often end up working with many of your own students as well.
2. Dr. Doitt does not show up for committee meetings.
3. Dr. Doitt does not keep his assigned, posted office hours.
4. Whenever the other faculty members in the department look for Dr. Doitt, he is "never around." He seems to come to campus only to teach his classes.
5. Dr. Doitt does not attend any social events or activities sponsored by the department, college, or university.

All these factors have brought your faculty members to the breaking point. Their heavy workload is affecting their teaching, research, and the quality of service they can give the students in your program. They tell you that they are all tempted to apply for jobs elsewhere. That last piece of information really catches your attention: these faculty members are very good and multiple searches in a year could be devastating to your small program. What do you do?

Questions

1. How do you communicate to Dr. Will Knott Doitt the problems that his behavior is causing in light of his passive-aggressive response to your earlier efforts?
   a. Would an intervention (a formal meeting in which you and the other members of the department confront Dr. Doitt with the problems his behavior is causing, reiterate your support for him personally, and insist that his behavior needs to change) be an effective communication strategy?
   b. Would involving the dean or a mediator in your conversation with Dr. Doitt be an effective strategy?
   c. Would developing a detailed performance plan be an effective strategy?

2. What is the most effective way of communicating with the faculty members who have brought their concerns to you?
3. Since your past experiences with mentoring Dr. Doitt were unsuccessful, would you attempt a mentoring approach again?
4. Would you respond any differently if Dr. Doitt were:
   a. A member of a racial minority?
   b. A woman?
   c. Severely physically challenged?
   d. Caring for a child with a chronic illness?
   e. Terminally ill?
   f. Untenured?
   g. An ineffective teacher who received poor student evaluations?
   h. Less collegial in his relationship with others?

Resolution

As the faculty members express their concerns to you, you listen carefully, trying to ascertain precisely what each person is saying—and feeling. When you reply to them, you relate specific concerns they have raised directly to the department's mission and goals. In other words, you are careful to distinguish between those behaviors that people merely find annoying and those that are actually causing serious hardship to the department. You also resolve to take several additional steps:

- No matter how much you feel that you yourself may be under attack, you decide that you will not become defensive if you believe your leadership is being questioned. You know that in tense communications in which people are venting about problems, they often direct their frustrations at their supervisors, even if they are not the people responsible for the problem. As criticisms of your leadership style occur, you consider whether each statement has merit, but you don't take it personally.
- Before the meeting ends, you will outline for the others what *process* you will use from this point forward, not necessarily what *decisions* are likely to result from that process. For instance, you decide to say something like, "I'm going to meet with Will next Wednesday and talk about what we've discussed here today. I'll be sure to give you an update by Friday."
- When the meeting with the faculty members is concluding, you will make sure that everyone understands your approach, even if not everyone agrees with it ("Okay, so do we all know what the plan is?"). You will underscore your commitment to act quickly on this matter.

You find the communication style of your dean, Dr. Pennon Teller, extremely difficult. Whenever she gives you and the other chairs a task to accomplish, she provides very vague instructions. No matter how hard you try to give her what she wants, she tells you that it is not right. As a result, you often have to redo each report and proposal four or five times before you finally figure out what she means. You feel as though she expects you to read her mind since her instructions seem clear to her but are completely unhelpful to you. The problem has recently come to a head because Dr. Teller asked you for a spreadsheet listing your priorities for faculty searches next year. You have already been through seven iterations of the spreadsheet, and Dr. Teller still is not happy. The last version was returned to you with a terse email message that simply said, "Not what I had in mind!!!!!"

Challenge Question: How do you guide the dean toward communicating with you in a more effective manner?

Scenario Outcome: You meet with Dr. Teller and explain to her, respectfully and constructively, why you believe that her communication style is not filling your needs. You explain that you are a very visual person and often need a model or a template in order to understand precisely how someone would like information organized. When she attempts to dismiss your concerns by saying, "You're merely asking me to do your own work for you. I don't have time for this. Every university in the world submits reports in the format I want them," you resist the urge to challenge her sweeping generalization and phrase your response more positively.

   "What I'm suggesting will actually *save* you time," you reply. "Until now, you've been having to send back my submissions repeatedly because I don't have a clear picture of what you want and how you want it. The short time it would take to draw up a template will, I believe, end up occupying less time in the future, and I know that it would be beneficial to several of my fellow chairs as well." As Dr. Teller considers that she does indeed have to send back most initial submissions not only to you, but to all the chairs in the college, she decides that you may have a point. Although her communication in many areas still continues to be excessively vague, she begins sending out samples of how she wants reports and proposals submitted to her. You find that the number of times you are asked to redo a submission drops considerably.

- You will end the meeting by expressing to each person your appreciation for his or her continued hard work and professionalism. You will also thank them each for bringing this to your attention.

Later, when you meet with Dr. Doitt, you begin by chatting informally with him. You are aware that in the meeting with the other three faculty members you only heard one side of the issue. Dr. Doitt may have a completely different (and possibly valid) perspective about the situation. You remind yourself to remain as objective as possible until you are certain that you understand the whole story. As Dr. Doitt responds to you, you take careful notes to ensure accuracy when you review these comments later. Even if you find Dr. Doitt's behavior totally inappropriate, you know that you will not lose sight of his strengths and overall importance to the department.

In your communications with Dr. Doitt, you try to indicate as specifically as possible where his behavior has been lacking and the negative effects it's having on students and his colleagues. Together the two of you consider developing a plan of action to help Dr. Doitt become a more valuable team player and a genuine asset to the department. The plan will include meetings between the two of you on a regular basis, detailing very specific tasks to be completed for each meeting, and a clear deadline for the completion of each task. The meeting ends on a positive note, even though you have made your expectations for future performance very clear.

ACTIVE LISTENING

Effective communication is not just about speaking and writing. It is also about listening carefully, considering the perspectives of others carefully, and seeing matters from their points of view. With active listening, we do not merely seek to understand the words a person is saying; we also try to grasp the underlying message behind those words, what the person is feeling, and the unspoken factors that have helped bring the person to his or her current state. Active listening involves strategies like the following:

1. *Observe body language.* Instead of focusing only on the words you are hearing, pay attention to what you are seeing too: What do the person's facial expressions, gestures, and posture tell you about how he or she is feeling right now? Nod occasionally, not necessarily to indicate that you agree with what the person is saying, but to signify that you are paying attention and to encourage the person to continue.

Lean slightly forward to signify that you are "in" the conversation, not pulled back and withdrawn.

2. *Reflect the person's feelings.* As a further indication that you are aware of the emotions the other person is experiencing, try to articulate how you would characterize those feelings. Say things like, "I know you're disappointed, and I believe you have every right to be" or "You seem frustrated by the bureaucratic delay." If you have correctly identified the person's emotional state, your comments will confirm to the other person that you are truly engaged in the conversation. If you have misidentified what the person is feeling, your remark provides the person an opportunity to correct any wrong impressions you have.

3. *Summarize the person's content.* People speak with their department chairs for a wide range of reasons. Sometimes they merely want to vent. At other times, they want a specific action taken. By summarizing occasionally what you believe the other person is saying, you are verifying that you are both on the same page and preventing yourself from taking action that the other person really does not want. You can say things like, "So what you're telling me is that you won't be able to give me a decision for at least two weeks" or "What you want me to do is call three of the students who attended the guest lecture, get their feedback, and let you know what I've learned no later than Wednesday afternoon."

4. *Ask for clarification where necessary.* Sometimes people have been dealing with a situation for so long that they believe issues are as clear to others as they are to them. If you are in any doubt about what a person means, simply ask politely for a clarification. Your question reinforces the idea that you are listening carefully and helps you avoid drawing any false conclusions. You can say things like, "Which enrollment numbers do you mean? As of today or at the end of the Drop/Add Period?" or "You just said that none of our proposals have been approved. But the faculty senate just endorsed our new degree plan, and the provost increased our travel budget. Which proposals did you mean? And at what level are you seeing this problem?"

5. *End with a clear action plan.* Even if a meeting has gone well, everything good that happened can be undermined if people leave with different impressions about what will occur next. It is often useful to wrap up a conversation with a summary built on the following formulas: "Okay, so just to clarify where we're going from here, I'm going to do [ACTION] by [DATE]. You're going to do [ACTION] by [DATE]. And we'll get back together on [DATE] to see how it's working out."

You are a new chair who has just been hired into your position from outside the institution. Since you have not been at your current university for very long, you have little or no knowledge of where the real power lies there. In the department you now lead, you have a faculty of nine full-time members. All of them are tenured, and each has been at the university for between eight and twenty-one years. At your previous university you saw firsthand how important it was to identify the key stakeholders and communicate effectively with them in order to accomplish everything that your discipline needed done.

These "opinion leaders" and power brokers were able to assist you in bringing many of your department's goals to fruition. In your new job you realize that you will need to establish good communications with key people very quickly so that you can continue the growth and well-being of your department. But since you are new, you have no idea whose advice you can trust, who is always looking out just for his or her own self-interest, and who talks a good game but rarely backs up those grandiose promises with action.

Challenge Question: What strategy do you use in order to promote effective communication with some key individuals at your institution when you have not yet even begun to understand the local politics?

Scenario Outcome: You decide to be proactive in discovering where you may need to build some bridges and what the communication styles of different people are. Within the department itself, you hold individual meetings with each of the nine full-time faculty members in your discipline. This approach gives you an opportunity to get to know them a bit better, understand what their concerns are, and pick up on the names that keep recurring in various conversations: those are the people with whom you will need to establish good communications first.

You want to be on the lookout for phrases like "But we *always* do it that way" and "We tried that before, and it didn't work." Expressions like these can be signs of departmental "hardening of the arteries" and an indication that your bridges outside the discipline may initially be of greater value than those within. You decide that your best plan of action is simply to keep your eyes open and refrain from too many commitments until you gain a better sense of the *type* of department you are now in.

Next you reflect on the question, "What are the *positions* at this institution that are absolutely critical to the success of my program?" Although you are aware that power does not always correspond with position, you believe that reflecting on people's assigned responsibilities offers you a good place to start. In most cases, the person who has the greatest influence on the welfare of a department is the dean. But you know you need to determine whether the dean is perceived as very weak or unpopular with the provost and president. You need to determine how much you can count on the dean's support.

You know from Robert Birnbaum's *How Colleges Work* that we develop a better understanding of the dynamics of a new department, college, or institution if we view it as a system: "Systems are hierarchical; they are made up of smaller systems and are themselves parts of larger systems. . . . We can understand a great deal about why institutions act as they do if we understand that they are responding to their perception of their environment" (Birnbaum 1991, 30, 42). For this reason, you start exploring how different people perceive their environment and what that perception tells you both about those people and the environment itself.

Finally, you investigate which person or office traditionally provides services to help newcomers to your institution get up to speed. Who is responsible for formal orientation or onboarding programs? Are those programs generally regarded as effective? Since these programs are usually run out of either the provost's office or the Office of Human Resources, they can provide you with keen insights into the key players at the university who are going to be most valuable to have in your communication chain.

CASE STUDY 4.3:
THE DEPARTMENT OF DESPAIR AND DESPERATION

You have recently become chair of the Department of Despair and Desperation at your institution. By all outward signs, your department appears to be doing quite well.

- The number of majors is at an all-time high, and your department's introductory courses regularly fill.
- While faculty salaries can always, of course, be higher, your department has made progress in recent years, and your area is on the verge of meeting the median salary of its aspirational group.

- Your department received a glowing reaccreditation report from DADA, the Despair and Desperation Accrediting group.
- Faculty scholarship is strong. Roughly one-third of your faculty publishes a book-length, peer-reviewed work each year. Income from grants has been high. Every faculty member is active in making conference presentations and publishing peer-reviewed articles regularly.
- Your discipline's internal program review recently received high scores from the institution in Quality, Sustainability, and Centrality to Institutional Mission.
- Faculty retention has been excellent. To the best of your knowledge, not a single faculty member is actively seeking employment elsewhere. No one has left the institution for another job for at least the past five years.

Despite these outward signs of success, however, everyone in your department seems to be complaining about most things most of the time. A recent institutionally mandated morale study indicated that your department currently ranks the lowest of the entire school both in overall morale and in its outlook toward the future. If some departments see the glass half full, and others see the glass half empty, the Department of Despair and Desperation is rapidly becoming known throughout your institution as the department that complains the glass is dirty, far too small to begin with, and never really given to them at all.

You quickly notice that this departmental attitude is taking a toll on your ability to accomplish your initiatives. No matter which course of action you recommend, you are met with an almost universal chorus of negativity. "We're working hard enough as it is," you're often told, followed by "Well, are you going to pay us more to do that?" You fear that, unless something is done to improve morale, the current strong student enrollment and other successes of your department cannot be sustained. What should you do?

Questions

1. How should you communicate with members of the department in order to determine the reasons for their poor morale?
2. Since the department is successful by most measures, should poor morale even be a serious concern?
3. With no more information than you have right now, can you think of ways of changing the negative atmosphere that appears to be rampant?

4. Suppose you learn that a leading cause of the department's problem is distrust of the administration, which means, by extension, you. How might you act on this knowledge?
5. Is there an effective way to advance your agenda despite the department's reluctance to change?

Resolution

You decide to hold a retreat off campus to discuss the continued viability of the department. You start by recognizing the individual achievements of each faculty member. You suggest that you are extremely proud of how well the department is doing and how honored you are to be part of it. Next you note that, in light of all these important accomplishments, you are starting a new webpage for the program that will highlight achievements as they occur and feature a different faculty member every month on a rotating basis. The webpage will be maintained by the department's administrative assistant, you announce, and will require absolutely no extra work from the faculty members themselves. Throughout the retreat you maintain a positive tone, at times rephrasing or reinterpreting sentiments expressed by other members of the program if they verge too far into negativity.

Following the retreat, you begin scheduling a number of celebrations as a regular part of the department's activities. You take care to celebrate, both formally at faculty meetings and informally at social gatherings, every sign of progress within the program. You make sure that everyone is aware of how important it is when someone receives tenure or promotion, has an article accepted for publication, submits a grant proposal, has a grant proposal funded, has a birthday, or reaches a personal milestone. At department meetings, immediately after the minutes are approved, you schedule a five-minute block of time for venting and complaints. You encourage people to purge their frustrations during this period and, once it is over, move on to current business with a more constructive outlook. If the atmosphere threatens to turn negative again, you lightly say, "I'm sorry but the Venting Period is over. That'll have to wait for the next meeting." In this way, people start to laugh at their own negativity and, in time, there is hardly any need for further venting periods.

You realize, however, that your plan requires a long-term commitment. You know you cannot eliminate the department's air of defeatism immediately. But you also know that, by refusing to yield to it yourself and by countering negative comments with evidence whenever you can, it will diminish eventually. The most important communication tool you have in your toolkit is modeling the behavior you most want others to adopt.

FACILITATION

Facilitation is a specific approach to communication in which leaders do not provide the message themselves, but instead serve as a catalyst for others to discover the message on their own. It is not appropriate in every situation but can be highly beneficial when there is a need for new ideas to be generated, a group to establish a better team identity, and members of the group to develop greater buy-in with a pending change.

In facilitation, leaders ask more questions than they answer. They adopt a Socratic method, helping the members of the program explore the consequences of various ideas and refine their own thoughts more precisely. By doing so, the leader tries to organize the discussion so that it will be more beneficial, not to force it into any particular direction. Facilitation can include such techniques as group brainstorming, assigning tasks to breakout groups, structured responses ("Dr. Smith, what do you think of the idea that Dr. Jones just proposed?"), and stacking (having people write ideas on note cards, shuffling the cards, and then considering each idea as that card is drawn).

At times during facilitation, leaders may feel like the stereotype of the therapist on television shows and in movies, asking "How do you feel about that?" or saying "Please tell me more about that." But as artificial as these devices may appear, they can actually be quite helpful in getting people to open up more, state objections to what others have said, and consider the implications of each idea in turn. Facilitation is particularly useful for:

- Problem solving
- Visioning
- Modeling new approaches
- Developing new processes
- Improving performance
- Managing conflict

The facilitator monitors the length of the discussion so that everyone has a chance to speak and that the conversation comes to fruition, intervenes if conflict begins to become negative, encourages those who are reluctant to speak, gently restrains those who want to speak too much, and helps the group summarize its conclusions. The facilitator never manipulates the situation to achieve the conclusion that he or she has foreordained, monopolizes the conversation, judges the adequacy of ideas as they are proposed, or makes the participants in the discussion feel uncomfortable or inadequate.

CASE STUDY 4.4: THE TOXIC TENURED TEACHER

A faculty member in your department of fourteen people, Dr. Crotchety, is a tenured full professor who has been at the university for more than thirty years. You have had a somewhat uneven relationship with Dr. Crotchety throughout your term as chair. At times he can display a very pleasant demeanor; when things go his way, he acts as though he is your best friend. But he can become quite vicious when he does not like a decision you have made.

For as long as you can remember, Dr. Crotchety has been scheduled to teach his classes on Tuesdays and Thursdays. There is no strong pedagogical reason for this arrangement; he merely liked this abbreviated schedule because it allowed him to be on campus only two days a week. This semester, however, you have had to change the course schedule in order to meet the enrollment demand created by the expansion of the university. As a way of fitting Dr. Crotchety's courses into the schedule along with several new courses, you have now had to assign him two classes on Mondays, Wednesdays, and Fridays, with one class taught on Tuesdays and Thursdays.

When Dr. Crotchety learns of the schedule change, he emails you a terse message indicating he wants to see you in your office tomorrow morning at 10:00 a.m. to discuss his teaching schedule. You fully anticipate an unpleasant meeting. At precisely 10:00 he storms into your office and begins shouting that you had no right to change the time and days of his courses. Although you try to explain the reasons for your actions, Dr. Crotchety becomes more and more belligerent. His complexion turns bright red, he gestures aggressively, and begins to give the impression "in your face" a much more literal meaning. You realize that you have to do something immediately to get the situation under control. What do you do?

Questions

1. Is this case one that lends itself to facilitation?
   a. If so, how would you organize the facilitation?
   b. If not, what factors of the case make facilitation unsuitable?
2. The case study tells you that Dr. Crotchety is one of fourteen faculty members in your department. Is there a way to enlist the other thirteen faculty to help you deal with this situation?
3. Would your response be any different if you knew that Dr. Crotchety were:
   a. In the midst of a painful divorce?

b. In therapy for anger management?
c. Arrested (though not convicted) for battery?
d. Your own mentor when you were a student?
e. About to retire in a few months?
f. Very friendly with your dean?

Resolution

As an immediate solution to the threatening posture Dr. Crotchety has taken in your office, you ask, "Do you mind if we go to the conference room? It's a bit cold in here." By doing so, you give Dr. Crotchety a few moments to calm down, remove yourself from the confined space in your office, and have an opportunity to leave the conference room door open so that, if the situation truly turns violent, others will hear, and there will be an open path for you to escape. Once you are both sitting down in the conference room, you ignore his earlier outburst and find common ground with Dr. Crotchety.

"Of course you're angry," you begin. "You have a right to be angry. I'd feel the same way if my schedule had been changed after so many years. In fact, I did feel that way once when a chair did exactly the same thing to me. But I know we both want what's best for the students and the program, and here's why I had to make this change . . ." You ask a few questions like, "What additional information can I provide you?" and "Would it be useful if together we could . . . ?" that give Dr. Crotchety a sense of control over the situation. While he is calmer during this discussion, he remains dissatisfied with your decision and, after a while, you feel that the conversation is no longer productive.

You decide to switch to a facilitation strategy. You conclude your conversation with Dr. Crotchety by saying that you will hold a mini retreat on the topic of how best to schedule courses in a way that fully meets the new enrollment demands you are facing. In this way, you will allow Dr. Crotchety to make his own case to the department, while also permitting his colleagues to point out any problems they see in that approach. You believe this strategy will be best for everyone. If together as a group people can reach a consensus that allows Dr. Crotchety to keep the schedule he wants, he will be happy, and you will have found a solution that you could not discover on your own. If Dr. Crotchety's proposal proves impossible, you will have multiple voices outlining the reasons why, not merely your own.

Being a good and experienced communicator, you try to maintain a proper balance between the emotional and the rational aspects of the situation. You empathize with Dr. Crotchety where you can. Instead of appearing accusatorial, you indicate the degree to which you can understand how he feels, saying things like:

- I appreciate your frustration.
- I understand your doubt.
- I share your concern.

At the same time, you guide the conversation away from purely emotional responses as necessary. You pose several factual questions, understanding that it is very difficult for people to remain angry when they are providing you with telephone numbers, catalogue numbers of courses, email addresses, and anything else that requires them to pause and recall a fact.

As academics, we are culturally conditioned to go into "analytical mode" whenever we are conveying information, and in your facilitation you are actually helping the group adopt a style of discourse in which people will be much less likely to say something they will regret later. Most importantly, you resolve to be open to whatever solution the facilitation produces. You know that the goal of a well-conducted facilitation process is to reach a workable consensus, not to impose your own ideas on others.

FOR REFLECTION

Without good communication skills, many of a chair's other strengths will be undermined. People may conclude that the chair is a poor leader based solely on their impressions, not reality. In addition, the chair runs the risk of ceding authority to those in the department who *are* effective as communicators and have no reluctance to express their points of view. Good communication takes practice, but even highly introverted people can become more effective in communication if they ask questions instead of primarily making statements, truly listen to both what a person is saying and how they are saying it, remain transparent about the reasons for their decisions, maintain good eye contact with others involved in the conversation, and model the type of communication style they hope others will adopt.

5

Managing Conflict

New department chairs are frequently surprised by how much time they spend managing conflict. There are conflicts between faculty members, between a faculty member and a student, between the faculty and staff, and between members of almost every set of stakeholders that an academic department has. Certainly, the principles we considered in the first four chapters of this book can help you *reduce* the amount of conflict you'll experience as a department chair, but you can't eliminate it entirely. Nor would you want to. There are two key principles that most department chairs find to be valuable when it comes to managing conflict:

1. Conflict is inevitable; incivility is optional.
2. Not all conflict is undesirable.

Let's consider how these principles apply to chairing an academic department.

Conflict usually occurs because people have incompatible desires for a limited resource. Two faculty members both want to be nominated for an award, but the department is only allowed to nominate one of them. A professor refuses to grant a student an excused absence even though the student believes she has a legitimate reason for missing the class. A faculty member wants an administrative assistant to drop what she's doing and help him meet an important grant deadline, while the administrative assistant believes the work you've assigned her as the chair is a higher priority. If one of these conflicts is ignored, it can cause many problems that affect productivity and the work environment throughout the discipline:

- Loss of time that could have been spent on more important issues.
- Departmental paralysis.
- Morale problems.
- Erosion of trust.
- Decreases in faculty research.
- Formation of polarized coalitions.
- Secrecy and reduced information flow.
- The triumph of negative emotions over reason and collegiality.
- Longstanding feuds.
- Destruction of departmental cohesiveness.

On the other hand, if a department never has any conflict at all, it can miss out on many of the *positive* effects that the right amount of internal tension can produce:

- Avoidance of groupthink.
- Generation of new ideas.
- Improved relations through compromise and negotiation.
- Spurred motivation resulting from people's desire to resolve the conflict.
- Clearer identification of where actual problems exist.
- Removal of people from their comfort zone.
- Necessary development of new knowledge and skills.
- Renewed creativity because conflict often compels people to consider new ideas.
- Catharsis when long-hidden tensions are brought into the light.

So simply avoiding all conflict isn't really in your department's best interests. It's more useful to avoid *negative and unnecessary conflict* by following the strategies we considered in chapters 1 through 4, and then *manage and profit from conflict* when it's unavoidable, desirable, or advantageous by adopting the strategies we'll consider in this chapter. So how do you do that? In *Getting to Yes: Negotiating Agreement Without Giving In*, Roger Fisher, Bruce Patton, and William Ury outline four strategies for successful conflict management:

1. Separate the people from the problem. As a way of decreasing the harshness of a dispute, it's helpful to focus the conversation on the issue itself, not the individual who's raising the issue. Instead of saying something like, "You're so inflexible. You always object to

new ideas," say instead, "The problem is that, if we don't at least try a new approach, we'll never know whether we can achieve better results." If you observe that other people are engaging in *ad hominem* attacks, you as the chair can gently guide them back to concentrating on the problem itself by saying things like, "Isn't what you're really saying that . . . ?" or "I think we can all agree that our real concern here is . . ."

2. Focus on interests, not positions. The positions people take in conflicts often stem from deeper needs or concerns, factors that Fisher, Patton, and Ury call *interests*. Suppose you have a conflict with a faculty member who refuses to relocate his lab even though you need his space for another program. His position is "I don't want to move," while yours is "I need you to move." But interests go deeper than that. The faculty member's interest might involve the potential disruption to his research, the time it will take to coordinate the move, or the convenience of the lab to his office. Your interest might stem from your desire to repurpose a space from a low-priority program to a high-priority program, your need to lower costs by locating the new program in that space, or the dean's directive that the new program *has* to be there. By identifying the true interests that lie behind the stated positions, a compromise or alternative solution may be possible.

3. Invent options for mutual gain. We tend to view conflicts as a zero-sum game. If one person "wins," someone else has to "lose." But by focusing on interests instead of positions, we can often create new options that result in a win-win situation. Suppose, for instance, that a geography program and a graphic design program each wants its own lab equipped with superfast computers and high resolution plotters, but you only have enough funding to supplement the budget of one of these disciplines. If you side with the geographers, the graphic designers "lose," and vice versa. But what if the geographers, the graphic designers, and you pool all of your resources into a single larger, better-equipped facility? Each discipline ends up with access to *far more sophisticated* equipment than they would otherwise had received, the space is better utilized, and no one "loses."

4. Insist on using objective criteria. Develop principles for resolving the conflict that reflect fundamental values rather than the personalities involved. If Fisher, Patton, and Ury's first strategy was to separate the people from the problem, their fourth strategy might be interpreted as "separate the people from the solution." For example, if your fundamental values are always to do whatever's in the best interests of the students, that commitment can guide you to a solution you can defend to all the parties involved. The best approach,

of course, is to decide what your fundamental values are *before* the conflicts arise, and then refer to them in finding solutions. You don't want to appear to be developing your "core values" ad hoc. The values of a department chair might include such principles as taking whichever course is likely to help student retention, promote undergraduate research, result in greater external funding, support the strategic plan, reduce costs, or whatever other principles you believe stand behind your administrative philosophy.

Based on Fisher, Patton, and Ury (2011), 17–41.

CASE STUDY 5.1: BUY MY NEW BOOK—OR ELSE

You're the chair of a department of sixteen full-time faculty members. You believe you have excellent and respectful relationships with all the faculty members in the department. Yesterday Dr. Dolittle, one of your faculty members, came into your office, closed the door, and said, "We have to talk about something right now. It could ruin our department!" With those words gaining your full attention, Dr. Dolittle went on to report that Dr. Watson, one of your tenured associate professors, had required students in each of the three courses she's teaching this semester to purchase her new, very expensive textbook.

The three courses all are taught at different levels of the discipline: one is a broad survey course, generally taken by first-year students; the second is an introduction to research techniques of the field, a course mostly populated by sophomores; and the third is a capstone preparation course, limited only to seniors. Dr. Dolittle thinks that requiring the same book for three very disparate groups of students is at best pedagogically unsound, at worse a serious breach of ethics and your discipline's professional code. He strongly suggests that, as the department chair, you must speak to Dr. Watson immediately and tell her that her requirement is not acceptable. "Dr. Watson can't use her position as professor to impose a requirement that brings her royalties. If word of what she's doing gets out, it'll be all over campus, maybe even in the *Chronicle of Higher Education*."

You set up a meeting with Dr. Watson to discuss Dr. Dolittle's concerns. About three sentences into your conversation, Dr. Watson becomes belligerent, demanding to know "Which one of my 'distinguished' colleagues thinks it's his place to interfere with my academic freedom? Let me tell you that textbook is the best thing out there for improving student research at each level of our discipline. That's why I wrote it, after all. You know they're just jealous." In the final analysis, Dr. Watson tells you that, since neither the university nor the department has any policy specifically prohibiting professors from assigning their own textbooks to students, she's completely within her rights to do whatever she wants. What do you do?

Questions

1. What is likely to be the result if you took each of the following actions?
   a. You refer the matter to the dean.
   b. You refer the matter to the college attorney.
   c. You hold a formal department meeting with both Dr. Dolittle and Dr. Watson to discuss the matter.
   d. You do nothing.
   e. You give a direct order that Dr. Watson assign other textbooks.
   f. You consult with other department chairs to gain insight into this dilemma.
2. We're told in the case study that the department has sixteen members. Do they have a right to weigh in on this issue? Or is it best handled administratively? What might be the result if you held a formal faculty meeting to discuss this issue?
3. To what extent do you consider this matter to be an issue of:
   a. conflict between faculty members?
   b. academic freedom?
   c. abuse of authority?
4. What alternatives might you propose that allow Dr. Watson to assign whatever textbook she likes, but that don't cause a conflict of interest because of the royalties involved?
5. Would it have made any difference in your decision if, instead of a tenured associate professor, Dr. Watson had been:
   a. an instructor?
   b. a tenure-track assistant professor in only her second year at the institution?
   c. a full professor with an international reputation for excellence in research?

Resolution

After listening to Dr. Dolittle and Dr. Watson, you find yourself asking, "How might my own actions have contributed to this problem?" In other words, you consider whether you yourself may have inadvertently caused a problem by failing to have created an appropriate policy to deal with this situation. As a result, rather than making the matter worse by exacerbating the conflict, you give Dr. Watson a chance to prove her claim that *one* textbook can be pedagogically appropriate for courses at *three very different* levels of your discipline.

You inquire whether she field tested material from the book before it was published and whether she has any data from those tests that would support her claim. At the same time, you act as a mentor to Dr. Watson and explain how different stakeholders at the institution may perceive her decision to assign her own textbook in all of her courses.

For instance, you note that trustees and parents of current students might see her action as an attempt to benefit financially from her students and note that their perception could harm the program. You discuss faculty/student power differentials from a general perspective and try to get her to see that her choice of textbook may be viewed as an attempt to coerce the students into paying her royalties.

You also keep the dean informed of this situation as the conflict may well spill over from the department to higher administrative levels. (Politically, you also want to know whether the dean "has your back" with regard to the approach you're taking.) You ask Dr. Watson whether her students couldn't gain more by learning the perspectives of different authors, since they receive her viewpoint in class anyway. Finally, you decide to appoint a taskforce that will develop an equitable policy for this type of situation in the future. Do you believe that this resolution will improve the situation, or will Dr. Watson merely regard you as having sided with Dr. Dolittle?

CASE STUDY 5.2:
THE DEPARTMENT OF CLIQUES AND FACTIONALISM

After leaving the Department of Despair and Desperation (see chapter 4), you accepted a new position as chair of the Department of Cliques and Factionalism. Although your interviews went well and everyone was extremely friendly before you were hired, shortly after your arrival in the department you noticed a disturbing trend. One by one, the various members of the discipline made appointments to see you. After a few of these conversations, it became apparent to you that your new department was being torn apart by political infighting. Each person was trying to win you over to his or her position, blaming most of the other department members for the difficulties the discipline had experienced.

For example, senior faculty members often said that the recent hires in the department were rude and unwilling to "pay their dues" before expecting to be praised and rewarded for their contributions to the discipline. The newer faculty members complained that those in the upper ranks were dismissive of important new trends in the discipline, attempted to impose standards on new hires that they themselves couldn't have met when they were younger, wished to control personal aspects of their colleagues' behavior (such as how a junior faculty member dressed, answered the phone, and greeted colleagues in the hallway), and demanded a level of respect that they had neither earned nor bestowed on others.

These problems wouldn't disturb you so much if they were the only concerns you had. But nearly every faculty member has also shared a long list of alleged or perceived grievances with you that he or she believes were suffered under previous chairs. They all want you to spend your time (and the department's resources) fixing the injustices of the past. Moreover, the various factions and allegiances in the department appear to be in constant flux.

One day a group of your faculty appears to be ganging up on one or two other faculty members for what they describe as inappropriate behaviors and lapses in judgment. Yet whenever you've tried to follow up on these allegations, the alliances always shift before you get very far. If one day you propose a solution to a problem that was brought to you the day before, you learn that the "crisis du jour" has changed. You're increasingly frustrated and not making headway on any of the initiatives you'd hoped to launch.

If it were not for its harm to your department's work and reputation at the institution, the situation would almost be comical. But others repeatedly characterize your new program as "dysfunctional," and you know that its productivity is suffering. What do you do?

Questions

1. Do you simply ignore the various charges and countercharges made within your department? If you ignore them, how do you respond when increasing numbers of your co-workers begin describing you as "worthless" because you "don't do anything" whenever they bring an issue to your attention?
2. Is there an effective way of dealing with the "generational" divide that appears to be present in your department?
3. Without initiating staff changes, how do you begin to change the culture of the department from one of mutual suspicion and accusation to one of trust, cooperation, and commitment to a common cause?
4. Do you institute any changes in policy or procedure in light of the situations you've inherited?

5. How do you deal with the perceived grievances of "past history" you've encountered?

6. Suppose you discovered that, due to a space shortage, a number of faculty members are sharing offices. After making a few inquiries, you discover that there's a correlation between office sharing and departmental factionalism. Is there an effective strategy to deal with this challenge?

    a. Does your strategy change if you learn that faculty members who share an office are likely to form a clique and "gang up on" others?

    b. Does your strategy change if you learn that faculty members who share an office are likely to get on one another's nerves and exhibit hostility toward one another?

    c. Does your strategy change if the dean tells you that the institution just doesn't have enough offices to give every faculty member his or her own?

Resolution

You decide to address this problem head on. What you want to do is to bring all these problematic behaviors to the surface, making it clear that your goal is to solve the problem, not to point fingers. You start by cautioning people not to name names during the discussion, but to be open and honest about the issues from a larger, more global perspective.

Your hope is that this conversation will result in a practical plan of action and a consensus about how to make the department a less hostile work environment. Your backup plan, if this strategy doesn't work, is to call on all the appropriate resources of the university (for example, the Office of Human Resources, Dean's Council, Counseling Office, and so on) and begin looking for a way to reshape how people in the department relate to one another.

For instance, you'll explore whether there are trained mediators or experts in organizational dynamics at the institution. If not, you'll inquire whether there is funding available to bring in external consultants who can view the problem more objectively. Finally, you decide to look for ways in which the department could begin making as many decisions as possible as a committee of the whole, without cliques, subcommittees, or other powerful groups.

In addressing the faculty, you say, "Despite whatever may have happened in the past, as chair I'll never cut private deals with individuals, even in cases where that might seem like the easiest option. We've all seen where this type of short-term thinking has gotten us, and these destructive practices have to end." Do you believe that this resolution will improve the situation, or will the department feel that you're blaming them for their past behavior?

FACTIONS AND THEIR ROLE IN CONFLICTS

Coalitions in departments sometimes seem like the mega-nations of Oceania, Eastasia, and Eurasia in Orwell's *Nineteen Eighty-Four* (1949): just when you think one alliance is fixed, suddenly yesterday's enemy becomes today's ally. At times, this situation results in a highly politicized environment in which faculty members begin to enjoy the sport of constant conflict. At other times, conflict arises because people have lost sight of what brings them together, but notice the forces that are pulling them apart. That problem can seem particularly severe when you're hired into a department from another institution.

You may be unaware of the unit's "baggage" (the history of relationships that affect people's views of one another) and not know where the "landmines" (the issues that cause people to "explode" as soon as you mention them) are. In these situations, the safest tactic is to proceed cautiously. At a meeting at which every member of the program is present, encourage them to identify the "elephant in the room" without placing the blame on anyone in particular, and then begin to work through the issues that have been so destructive. Look for ways to discourage attempts by the faculty to negotiate backroom deals with one another, deprive the coalitions of their perceived power, and establish a new operating procedure for the department to use in the future.

One way of achieving this goal would be to initiate a few minor procedural changes. For instance, declare your own moratorium on meeting with individuals or small groups on any but the most private issues. While you may not believe that this strategy is a good idea for the long run, doing so temporarily might break the department's chain of destructive behaviors. It offers you a chance to "reboot" the culture of the department.

The secret that many chairs don't learn until many years on the job is that not every new policy has to be a permanent policy. In higher education, we often place far too much emphasis on precedent and "the way we've always done things around here." We need to remember sometimes that, unlike individuals, policies don't receive "tenure"; we put them in place for as long as they work and, as soon as they stop working, we develop new policies.

As a longer-term solution, it can be helpful for you as chair to make a commitment that you'll practice complete transparency in all departmental decisions. When it's clear that someone's about to share with you some "confidential information" (which is more likely gossip anyway), mention that your own policy of candor may require you to share what you're told with the rest of the department. That will circumvent attempts to pull you into one faction over another.

CASE STUDY 5.3: TAKING THE JOB, BUT NOT DOING THE JOB

You're a chair at an institution where one of your duties is to appoint directors for the various programs that exist within your department. Although the faculty members in that area may *recommend* their preferred candidates, the decision about who the director will be is ultimately up to you. In your Program on Passive-Aggression, there is only one faculty member, Dr. Bitter, in whom you have confidence as a candidate for the director position. In your mind, every other member of the program is either too unwilling to work effectively for the administration, too disengaged, or too unpredictable to be in any way acceptable to you as an administrator. For this reason, you've appointed Dr. Bitter to several two-year terms as director, including the term that's just begun.

For the most part, your relationship with Dr. Bitter has been excellent—until the last few weeks. During a job search, the program was unanimous in recommending one candidate for the job, declaring all the other finalists unsuitable. You, however, were concerned that the search committee selected its candidate largely because she was almost identical in research focus, outlook, and personality to all the current members of the program.

But you had a different goal in mind for this search: you wanted the program to grow, to start doing things a bit more creatively, and to consider new ideas. The program, in your opinion, was becoming stagnant, and its lack of energy was being reflected in declining student enrollments and an unsatisfactory record of research productivity. Your own preferred candidate was another finalist who, in your opinion, could not only move the program in a bold new direction, but also bring some much-needed ethnic diversity to the institution.

You've discussed the issue at length with Dr. Bitter, the search committee, and the entire discipline—all to no avail. In your mind, their arguments in favor of their preferred candidate seemed weak and superficial, while their resistance to the other candidate appeared based on emotion, not reason. Finally, although you were reluctant to do so, you felt the issue had reached such an impasse that you ignored the search committee's advice and recommended that the dean offer a contract to the candidate you believed to be better suited to the job. The dean took your recommendation, and your preferred candidate was hired.

Dr. Bitter showed up in your office the next morning. "Here's my letter of resignation as director of the Program on Passive-Aggression," he
began. "I can't work with a chair who questions my professional judg-
ments the way you did yesterday." Once again you tried to discuss the
issue calmly with Dr. Bitter, pointing out the reasons why you preferred
the other candidate and urging him to stay on as director. None of your
arguments affect him in the slightest.

Finally you say, "Look, I've got a real problem here. There's simply
no one else in the program who can function as director. I *need* you to
stay on." You've known Dr. Bitter long enough that you feel you can
trust him: you go through each person in the discipline one by one,
pointing out why that person would be harmful to the program and the
institution.

"All right," Dr. Bitter said, taking back his letter. "I'll keep the job; I
simply won't *do* the job." At first you thought he was joking, but he's
been as good as his word. Ever since your meeting, Dr. Bitter has stopped
attending your weekly department meetings. Your emails to him have
gone unanswered. He has continued to submit the schedule for the program and has completed all the minor tasks that allowed courses to run
and the program to function, but he hasn't done a single thing more.

You have appointed Dr. Bitter to various committees; he never
attended. You left him stern voicemails on his phone; he never returned
your calls. You're tempted to dismiss him from the director's position, but
then you recall that there's no one else in the discipline who would make
a suitable replacement. What do you do?

Questions

1. Suppose you decide to try mending your relationship with Dr. Bitter
   so as to resolve this impasse. What would you say to him? Where
   would you hold the conversation? What would you regard as nego-
   tiable and what would be non-negotiable?
2. Suppose you decide that you've "had it with his insubordination."
   What punitive steps do you think would be justified? How do you
   take those steps without punishing yourself worse than Dr. Bitter?
3. Suppose you decide to name another member of the program as
   director, even if that person is unsuitable. What steps should you
   take in order to avoid a worse problem than the one that already
   exists?
4. Suppose you decide to place the program in receivership and
   appoint a director from another academic area. What steps would
   you take to make this option proceed as smoothly as possible?

5. Whom else might you want to talk to about this matter in order to resolve it?
6. To what extent do you feel that you were responsible for this problem in the first place?

Resolution

You decide that Dr. Bitter is acting in an immature and spiteful manner, but you're loath to replace him because even greater problems are likely to result if you do. To try to remedy the situation: you assign another successful program director to serve as Dr. Bitter's mentor and to guide him in more effective ways of dealing with his differences with you.

You decide that you'll give this plan one year to work. If it doesn't, you intend to merge the Program on Passive-Aggression with the more successful Program on Outright Hostility, assigning a single director to the entire unit. Do you believe that this resolution will improve the situation, or is one of the following unintended consequences more likely to occur?

1. The Program on Outright Hostility, which was getting along reasonably well previously, then becomes infected with the negativity of their new colleagues and the combined unit proves to be increasingly resistant to your leadership.
2. The new faculty member that you forced the program to hire doesn't work out (perhaps because Dr. Bitter and his colleagues never gave this person a fair chance), proving to those in the discipline that "We were right all along."
3. Your reputation at the institution becomes diminished as a chair who doesn't listen to the faculty.
4. Your dean concludes that you created the entire problem yourself because of your stubbornness about the hire and decides to appoint Dr. Bitter as the new chair.

MODEL THE BEHAVIOR YOU WANT FROM OTHERS

As chairs, we may not always think of ourselves as role models. But the faculty, staff, and students in our areas take their cues from us in terms of what an acceptable response to conflict might be. With this principle in mind, when you find yourself in a situation that seems to be escalating, there are several things you can do to guide the conflict in a more positive direction:

- Ask everyone involved in the discussion to sit down, if they happen to be standing, and seek a place to talk that is private but spacious enough that no one feels crowded.
- As each person speaks, demonstrate active listening by nodding occasionally, leaning slightly toward that person to demonstrate

---

Two longstanding faculty members in your area have had a conflict that dates back many years. To the greatest extent possible, you have simply tried to avoid creating situations you think will be likely to result in overt hostility. You've ensured that their offices are as far apart as possible. You've avoided putting them on the same committees. You've even developed a course schedule that reduces the chance they'll run into one another on a regular basis.

Challenge Question: What do you do if the dean assigns both of these faculty members to the same small taskforce and, despite your reservations, they really are the two best people for the job?

Scenario Outcome: People don't keep a conflict going year after year unless they're invested in it for some reason. In this case, the two faculty members must feel that they're getting something valuable from the conflict. What each person is getting out of the situation could be a matter of self-image ("*I'm* the one who supports high academic standards around here, not like *that person*."), hurt feelings ("I still can't believe that that person didn't support my promotion fifteen years ago."), past history ("I once went out with that person, and it ended badly. What was I thinking?"), or something else. To whatever extent possible, a suitable outcome begins with trying to determine *why* the two people are so invested in this conflict and whether you can satisfy that need *in some other way*.

Remember, too, the four strategies of Roger Fisher, Bruce Patton, and William Ury that were summarized earlier in this chapter. Try to look beyond the personalities involved and the positions they are taking to see what their underlying interests are. See if you can provide some positive reinforcement for them to put aside their differences, at least until the taskforce completes its charge, and to work together for a goal they both care about. Longstanding conflicts of this sort are resistant to being resolved, but it's possible that, by establishing a few conflict-free ground rules with these faculty members, they may discover a new operating procedure for working with one another.

One faculty member in your department has a reputation for getting along with everyone. She's the person people often go to for advice, and she always remembers everyone's birthday and other special occasions. Over the course of the current semester, however, you've noticed a gradual change. She's increasingly become short-tempered with her colleagues, and even a few students have complained to you about her impatience when they make the sort of mistakes that are a regular part of the learning process. Finally, after making several very cutting remarks to junior faculty members in a meeting, she slammed down a book when she was challenged on a minor point, announced "I don't need to put up with this!" to no one in particular, and stormed out of the room.

Challenge Question: How do you deal with this situation as a chair now that a number of her colleagues and students are being affected by her behavior?

Scenario Outcome: This scenario is difficult for a number of reasons. First, the faculty member's behavior has changed so dramatically that it doesn't appear to be typical for her. Something serious has happened, either in the way someone (perhaps in the department, perhaps in her private life) has treated her or due to another cause, such as a health condition. Second, you don't want to make assumptions about what the problem is because, regardless of whether your conclusion is right or wrong, her response might exacerbate the situation and cause her to no longer trust you as an honest broker.

One strategy might be to talk to her, calmly and without assigning blame, in the privacy of her office. Mention that you've noticed how her behavior has changed and that you are concerned. If your institution has an Employee Assistance Program, mention that there are resources available that can help her if she would like to make use of them and that all you want is what is best for her. If even your gentle reference to the situation prompts an angry response, reiterate that your greatest concern is her welfare, resist any temptation you may have to respond angrily ("I was only trying to help!"), and keep your supervisor and Office of Human Resources informed about the situation.

You notice that two faculty members in your department are not speaking to one another. In fact, both go out of their way to avoid one another. During department meetings they tend to be very negative toward one another and to discount any suggestions the other person makes. You also notice that this behavior has made the rest of the department feel uncomfortable and less willing to participate in the meetings. Later, you discover that the conflict between the two faculty members stems from differences in teaching philosophy. Their behavior is stifling the productivity of a department committee on which both serve as members.

Challenge Question: How will you handle this situation?

Scenario Outcome: You meet separately with each of the two faculty members and say, "Lately I've noticed that there seems to be tension between you and your colleague. I don't want to pry into personal matters but, as your chair, I'm concerned about certain ways in which the department seems to be suffering as a result." You mention several problems that have occurred lately," being careful to focus only on the behavior, not the person, and to avoid assigning blame. While you initially met some resistance and attempts at self-justification, eventually each faculty member admitted that the quarrel had begun to hamper the work of the discipline and agreed to meet together with you and the other faculty member.

When the three of you are together, you start by saying "We're not here to change anyone's mind or to find fault with anyone for anything done in the past. What we're here for is to develop an operating agreement for the future. We need to find a way to work effectively with one another so that our students and the other faculty members in the program can thrive. Now, what I suggest is this . . ." You outline some basic principles like setting aside personal issues for the duration of a committee meeting and making a commitment not to draw other people into the dispute. The discussion goes on for nearly two hours, but you come away from it convinced that the quarrel, although not solved, will now be far less likely to cause lasting damage to your program.

Cheryl is your department's administrative assistant. Tom serves as your associate chair. One day at 4:00 p.m., Tom gave Cheryl a document to complete that he said was of the utmost importance. It is well known throughout the department that Cheryl regularly leaves work at 4:30 p.m. to pick up her children from daycare. In her haste to get Tom the document he needed before she left that day, Cheryl inadvertently omitted an important spreadsheet.

The next morning you observe that Tom is standing in front of Cheryl's desk, angrily blaming her for the mistake. "How could you be so stupid?" you hear him ask. "Don't you ever read what you're working on? The way you screw things up, I don't know why we bother to keep you." Cheryl is visibly upset. She is a naturally shy person and now is embarrassed because everyone in the office, including students and another administrative assistant, saw Tom's reaction.

Challenge Question: How should you handle this situation?

Scenario Outcome: At the earliest opportunity, you pull Tom aside and explain, calmly but assertively, that his outburst to Cheryl was unacceptable. You explain that everyone in the department is doing his or her best and that, while all of us make occasional mistakes, none of those mistakes is intentional. You remind Tom of how many times Cheryl has helped him in the past, explain that she puts in a lot of hours for a salary that is significantly less than his, and will not respond positively to the abuse he's given her. You note that, as chair, you are the one who supervises Cheryl and that, if there are concerns about her performance, you'll be the one to address them. Although it takes a long time for Tom to calm down, he finally begins to understand that he overreacted and publicly apologizes to Cheryl, taking full responsibility for his anger.

interest, and occasionally paraphrasing each person's point of view to make sure that you (and everyone else present) understands what the real issues are.
- Maintain an open posture by not crossing your arms or legs in a way that seems to suggest your mind is already closed to new ideas.
- Speak softly, calmly, and slowly.
- Make eye contact with each speaker, but don't stare or glare at anyone.

You learn that while you were at a meeting, two of your faculty members, Chris Johnson and Taylor Ford, got into a heated argument in the hallway. The issue they were quarreling about had to do with a student's right to appeal a grade. As soon as you learn of the incident, you decide that you'll have an informal conversation with each faculty member individually in order to understand the issue better. But while you're in Taylor Ford's office inquiring about the incident, Chris Johnson walks in and is angry, not just with Taylor, but now with you for "letting Taylor give you one side of the story first."

Challenge Question: How should you handle this situation?

Scenario Outcome: You calmly explain to Chris that it's your intention to hear the story from each of them and that you just happened to reach Taylor's office first. You ask Chris to give you some privacy with Taylor and say that you'll come over to the office in fifteen minutes. You tell both of the faculty members that once you've had private conversations with each of them you'd like all three of you to get together to talk about what happened. You note your support of people's rights to disagree with one another, and you commend their passion, but say that you just want to make sure that you're all handling the conflict in the most positive way possible. With that said, you return to your conversation with Taylor and follow-up with Chris, as you promised, fifteen minutes later.

Follow-Up Question: The names Chris and Taylor in this scenario were intentionally selected to make the gender of the two faculty members ambiguous. Which gender did you assume each character to be? Might you have handled the conflict any differently if each person were of the other gender?

- Avoid any activity that can intensify the air of hostility in the room: pointing at someone, rolling your eyes (no matter how unreasonable someone may be), tapping your fingers, waving your hands dismissively, clenching your fists, or checking the time.

FOR REFLECTION

The best time to manage a potentially destructive conflict is ⸃ᵣ.ᵉ it begins. For this reason, it's often helpful for chairs to use a departmental retreat or the first faculty meeting of the year to establish some basic guidelines for interaction among colleagues. Some programs may even decide to establish a "departmental code" for how they will air disagreements with one another. All departments are different, and ground rules that one discipline finds very helpful may not work at all in a different environment. Here are a few possible guidelines from which your department may draw in developing its own policy on airing disagreements:

- We will discuss differences of opinion openly, and we will grant everyone an opportunity to be heard.
- Members of the department will be free to express their views on a subject without fear of interruption or retaliation.
- We will make the utmost effort to substantiate our assertions with evidence.
- We will respect one another as professionals. When we disagree, issues and not personalities will be the subjects of our debate.
- We will refrain from using abusive language even when we feel frustrated or annoyed by the actions of others.
- We understand that, as faculty members, we care deeply about many issues. We recognize that, from time to time, the intensity of our discussions may result in tears or emotional outbursts. While those reactions are perfectly valid, we understand that they should not derail the reasoned and considered discussion of substantive issues.
- Issues that affect the entire department will be discussed and decided openly at department meetings and not by any subgroup of the faculty.
- We agree to disagree without being disagreeable.

6

Making Decisions

Making decisions as a department chair can sometimes feel like trying to negotiate your way through a minefield. If you succeed, you survive—only to face the next minefield that lies ahead. If you fail, there is an explosion that causes an amazing amount of destruction. In the case of your work as a chair, that "explosion" can damage your department's credibility, morale, and productivity. In a worst-case scenario, it can harm you professionally. So there is a lot at stake in the quality of your decisions.

One of the most important frameworks for any decision you make as a chair will be the mission of your institution, college or school, and department. A good touchstone for any decision you have to make, therefore, is to ask yourself, "How will this decision help or hinder my department's efforts to fulfill its mission?" As a result, the decision you make if your program has a strong research mission may well be quite different than if you are chairing a service department at a teaching institution.

In addition to mission, your framework for making decisions must also include existing policies and procedures. Even though the very thing that you are deciding may be to waive one of those policies and procedures, the fact that they exist in the first place affects the choice you are about to make. By deviating from past practice, you are setting a precedent that will guide others in their future actions. So every time you make an exception to the rules, it is important to consider what additional consequences may arise from the choice you have made.

The third element of your decision-making framework should be the major goals of your strategic plan and any particular challenges your program may be facing. For example, if your department has been under pressure to boost enrollment, then that goal also provides you with guidance about how you should proceed. Taken as a whole, then, a valuable framework for making decisions at the departmental level would be to ask the following three questions:

1. How will this decision help or hinder my department's efforts to fulfill its mission?
2. How is this decision affected or guided by existing policies and procedures?
3. How might the choice I make help me either to advance a strategic goal or solve a pressing problem?

CASE STUDY 6.1: WHO TEACHES WHAT—AND WHY?

You have been very fortunate to secure the services of a rising young star in your field, Dr. Newcomer, who has already proven to be a fine and popular teacher. Student course evaluations say that Dr. Newcomer is engaging, exciting, and very student-centered in class. As chair, you have attended several of Dr. Newcomer's classes (since your policies require you to sit in occasionally on the courses of all professors in their first two years), and it is very clear to you that this is a phenomenal young instructor who cares deeply about the students and wants them to excel. What particularly impressed you is that Dr. Newcomer presents the latest research in your field in innovative ways, using a variety of teaching methods that address multiple learning styles.

Even while teaching a fairly heavy load, Dr. Newcomer also serves on three department committees, two college committees, and three university-wide committees. Dr. Newcomer holds a terminal degree from one of the leading programs in your field and, at the time you conducted the search, was just completing a very prestigious post-doc. On the whole, therefore, you feel very fortunate that you have Dr. Newcomer on your faculty and pride yourself on having hired precisely the right person.

Also on your faculty is Dr. Relic, who has been in the department for thirty-seven years, the last twenty-four of which included teaching a research course that is a requirement for all your graduate students. Dr. Relic is not a very stimulating teacher and, for the past four years, has received steadily declining course evaluations. On the other hand, Dr. Relic is generally liked by the rest of the department and, after such a long period of service to the institution, is generally treated with a great deal of respect. Although no specific announcement has been made, you assume that it will not be very long before Dr. Relic retires.

You have been so concerned about this decline in teaching effectiveness that, during last year's evaluation, when you mentioned several student complaints to Dr. Relic, the response you received was uncharacteristically defensive and peevish. "Can't you tell what's really going on here? We just haven't been recruiting top-tier students. The ones we get are lazy, unmotivated, and unlikely to succeed in our field. I'm not like these new professors—What's the name of the latest one? Newcomer?—who have very low standards, give everyone an A, and curry favor with students just to get good evaluations. I have my pride, you know."

One day, five other members of your department ask to meet with you. They are very concerned about the quality of Dr. Relic's teaching and feel that it is getting in the way of student success in their own courses. "When we get them, they expect to do research like it was done twenty years ago. Maybe even more. They don't know anything about current methods, and we end up having to teach them techniques from scratch." What they request is for Dr. Newcomer to be assigned the graduate research course instead. They insist that they do not dislike Dr. Relic and that their request is not personal. They simply believe that it is in the best interests of the program.

The more you reflect on the situation, the more you find yourself agreeing that Dr. Newcomer would do a much better job with this class. Your one reservation is how Dr. Relic will respond if you reassign the course. As chair, you also have Dr. Newcomer's future to think about: Dr. Relic could be a strong advocate or a terrible enemy when it comes time for Dr. Newcomer's tenure and promotion decision. Even worse, as you think through the rotation, you realize that Dr. Relic will actually be the head of the department's personnel committee when Dr. Newcomer is reviewed. Dr. Relic is a close friend of several people who serve on the college- and university-level personnel committees, too, and you know that alienating Dr. Relic could have far reaching effects. What do you do?

Questions

1. What is likely to be the result if you decide to:
   a. Tell Dr. Relic that Dr. Newcomer will begin teaching the graduate research course next semester?
   b. Have Dr. Relic and Dr. Newcomer meet and try to work out a plan themselves?
   c. Refer this decision to the dean?
   d. Discuss the issue at a faculty meeting and have people give you their recommendation by anonymous ballot?
   e. Allow Dr. Relic to continue teaching the course?

2. Would your decision be any different if:
   a. Dr. Relic were scheduled to retire in two years?
   b. The college and university personnel committees had a tradition of only approving candidates for tenure and promotion who had the unanimous support of their departments?
   c. Your department and institution had a strong teaching mission?
   d. Your department and institution had a strong research mission?
   e. Graduate enrollment in your department had been declining and you had been instructed by the dean to "do something about it"?
   f. Dr. Newcomer did not have as strong a record in research as in teaching and service?
   g. This were Dr. Newcomer's fifth or sixth year of service instead of only the second?
3. If you decide to assign the course to Dr. Newcomer, do you do so primarily because:
   a. Several valued members of your faculty have made this request?
   b. You hope to improve student success by this decision?
   c. No one should ever "own" a course?
   d. It is easier for you to live with this decision?
4. If you decide to let Dr. Relic continue teaching the course, do you do so because:
   a. After so many years of loyal service, Dr. Relic deserves to teach this class?
   b. Dr. Newcomer will eventually have a chance to teach the course, and Dr. Relic cannot be long from retirement anyway?
   c. Faculty members essentially "own" the courses they have taught for a long time?
   d. It is easier for you to live with this decision?

Resolution

You and other members of the department are all in agreement that Dr. Newcomer is currently the best person to teach this important required course. You have reservations, however, that if you make this decision, there will be serious problems ahead. Right now your relationship with Dr. Relic is fairly good, but you've had a taste of this professor's irritable side and feel that Dr. Relic is capable of making everyone's life miserable if provoked. More importantly, you recognize that Dr. Newcomer's tenure status could be compromised by this decision.

Four factors are at work in your decision making:

1. As an academic leader you know how destructive it can be to embarrass anyone. There are always face-saving ways to deliver

unpleasant news, and you would like to handle this situation in a way that preserves the dignity of Dr. Relic.

2. Since Dr. Relic is nearing retirement, leaving a legacy is likely to be an important concern. People almost always want to be remembered fondly for their positive accomplishments.

3. Department chairs have a responsibility to look out for the interests of *all* their faculty members. Even for those who are senior to you, you feel you have a duty to serve as a role model and mentor, helping them reach goals that are good both for themselves and for the program.

4. Department chairs are most likely to make mistakes when they rush to make a decision. In your time as chair, you have learned that it is far better to take your time, look at all the possible consequences of your decision, and make certain you have all the facts.

You decide, therefore, to proceed with care and keep the matter as low-key as possible. You invite Dr. Relic out for lunch at a quiet restaurant off campus. There, in the course of the conversation, you begin to lay out a few of your ideas for the future of the program. You also ask how Dr. Relic would like to be remembered by the department. As you expect, Dr. Relic takes great pride in the graduate research class and wants to see it thrive. You inquire, therefore, whether Dr. Relic could begin mentoring Dr. Newcomer to carry on the success of that course eventually. Perhaps, you suggest, Dr. Newcomer could even start team teaching the course in order to gain more hands-on experience and also to relieve Dr. Relic of such a heavy workload.

Although you do not say it, you hope that Dr. Newcomer's talent as a teacher will start raising the bar for Dr. Relic, or at least clear the way for Dr. Newcomer to take over the course in the near future. Dr. Relic does

---

Two of your faculty members, Dr. Yeller and Dr. Hollar, both want to attend an important national conference. Your problem is that your university has just undergone a massive budget cut and travel funding has been almost entirely eliminated. By pooling funds from other sources, you calculate that you can send one of them but not both. You have very little basis to decide between them. Both are tenured associate professors with the same number of years in the department. Since the conference is so significant, you feel it is a priority for one of them to attend, but that requires you to decide between two very deserving choices.

Challenge Question: How do you go about making a fair, unbiased, and well-informed decision?

Scenario Outcome: You conclude that, if one of them were either an assistant professor or a full professor, your decision would be easier. You want assistant professors to attend conferences to better position themselves for tenure and promotion, and a full professor could be given preference over an associate professor on the basis of seniority. But your current predicament does not provide you with these options.

The best solution would be, of course, to develop a policy on how to handle this kind of situation when you did not have an actual case in front of you. In that way, your judgment would not be affected, even subconsciously, by your feelings about Dr. Yeller and Dr. Hollar. So you decide to do the next best thing. You decide to base your decision on factors that you do not currently know. All you are aware of so far is that both of them want to attend the conference. In order to decide the issue, you decide that the following will be your priorities. Whichever of the two faculty members meets the criterion with the lowest number will be the person who will receives the money.

1. Someone who is presenting a keynote address.
2. Someone who is delivering a presentation other than a keynote address.
3. Someone who is an officer in the organization. (If both are officers, the one with the higher rank will be given preference.)
4. Someone who is serving as a respondent on a panel.
5. Someone who is introducing speakers on a panel.
6. Someone who is presenting research in a poster session.
7. The person who has not attended this conference for the longest time.
8. The person who has not attended *any* conference for the longest time.

Only after you set these priorities do you begin to ask Dr. Yeller and Dr. Hollar about them. When you do so, you discover that the first four criteria do not apply to either of them. However, Dr. Yeller will be introducing speakers on a panel while Dr. Hollar will not. You give the money to Dr. Yeller.

not initially warm to the idea, but as you continue to outline how such a plan will benefit Dr. Relic, you sense that you are achieving the purpose and leave the lunch with a clear plan for Dr. Relic to begin handing over the course to Dr. Newcomer.

GENERAL PRINCIPLES FOR GOOD DECISION MAKING

In addition to the three-framework approach mentioned earlier—paying attention to mission, current policies, and important goals or problems—what tools do department chairs need in their toolkits in order to make the best possible decisions for their programs? We believe there are five:

1. *Integrity.* Nothing undermines a chair's credibility more than the perception that a decision was made to benefit a particular person or faction rather than the program as a whole. What is sometimes called *authentic leadership* involves making decisions on the basis of consistent, defendable values. Demonstrating partiality rather than conviction not only protects your integrity, but also protects you from setting poor precedents you will have to live with later.
2. *Consistency.* That same consistency of values that helps preserve your integrity also assists your decision making in other ways. While Emerson's oft-quoted remark that "a foolish consistency is the hobgoblin of little minds" means that we should not be inflexible as academic leaders, it does not justify unpredictability either. The members of the department (not to mention your dean and fellow chairs) expect that you will generally follow the course that you set. Making too many exceptions can be just as bad as making no exceptions at all. A major reason for institutions to have administrators is for there to be someone to decide when allowances are warranted. If you never grant an exception, the department does not need a chair, just a rulebook. If you always grant exceptions, the department does not need a chair because there are no rules to enforce.
3. *Proactivity.* When we make decisions as a reaction to a problem that has occurred, we tend to enter crisis mode. We want to repair whatever damage has occurred, and in order to do so quickly, we usually make decisions with less reflection, consultation, and information gathering than we would otherwise. Being proactive in decision making means conducting a scan of the department on a regular basis to see where problems are likely to arise and whether they can be prevented.

4. *Inclusiveness.* As we just saw, one of the dangers of having to make quick decisions is that we are more likely to make them in a vacuum. Including others is our decision-making process has many benefits. It gives us the advantage of learning from the wisdom of others, promotes their buy-in when the decision is made, prevents people from feeling blindsided by an unexpected decision, and sends the message that you are not the type of leader who sets policies behind closed doors.

5. *Transparency.* Being inclusive is one way of being transparent in our decision making. But transparency also includes revealing to people the principles and process you used to arrive at a decision, the type of information you considered, the alternatives you explored, and the reasons that led you to choose one option over another. Not everyone will agree with each decision you make, but transparency will assure others that their voices were heard and your process was reasonable.

CASE STUDY 6.2: THAT'S MY PARKING SPACE!

As chair of the Department of Effective Decision Making, you work alongside seventeen full-time faculty members, one administrative assistant, two graduate assistants, and four adjuncts. The department has its own small building right beside a parking lot with twenty-eight numbered spaces. In the eight years you have occupied the building, you have found it to be perfectly suited to your needs: in addition to offices for all the faculty and staff, it has the classrooms, labs, and seminar facilities you need to run your program.

In a meeting with your dean, you are surprised to learn that a new facility for the Department of Hostile Takeovers will break ground *next week* on the other side of "your" parking lot. That department currently consists of a chair, an administrative assistant, eleven full-time faculty members, eight graduate assistants, and nine adjuncts. You have had a good working relationship with the chair of the Department of Hostile Takeovers for many years. While the two of you do not socialize outside of work, you do share a mutual respect for each other and have gotten to know each other through work on several committees.

Your immediate concern is that "your" parking lot, the only one the institution has within a mile of your building, has simply too few spaces to accommodate everyone in both departments. In fact, it is too small even to serve every member of the Department of Hostile Takeovers. You worry about the inevitable complaints from the faculty and staff, but you are even more worried about how the lack of parking spaces will affect your program. Students have a hard time reaching you now; what will happen when even the few unused spaces are gone? You ask the dean whether additional parking will be included with the new building and are told that it will not be. There simply is no funding available to increase the size of the lot. What do you do next?

Questions

1. What decision, if any, do you make before leaving the dean's office?
2. What is likely to be the outcome if you make each of the following decisions?
   a. You explain the problem to the dean and ask for it to be solved at the dean's level, since that is where it was caused.
   b. You meet with the chair of the Department of Hostile Takeovers, point out that your department was there first and you have first claim to all the spaces in the parking lot.
   c. You tell the chair of the Department of Hostile Takeovers that you will "give them" eight of the twenty-eight parking numbered spaces because you are a nice person.
   d. You split the lot with the other department so that you each have fourteen spaces to allocate however you see fit.
   e. You split the lot with the other department proportionally (thirteen spaces for your department, fifteen spaces for the other department) based on the total number of people who work in both programs.
   f. You split the lot with the other department proportionally (seventeen spaces for your department, eleven spaces for the other department) based on the total number of full-time faculty members (including the chairs) in both departments.
   g. You have people draw names at random for the right to have a parking space.
   h. You give the twenty-eight most senior people in both departments the right to have a parking space.
   i. You switch to a system in which no one has an assigned parking space, and the lot becomes first come/first served.
   j. You consult a parking engineer to learn whether more spaces might be added to the lot if it were configured differently.
3. What other information would you like to have before making a decision?
4. Would any of the following changes to the case study cause you to make a different decision?

a. Rather than having a good working relationship with the chair of the Department of Hostile Takeovers, the two of you have a very poor relationship. You view the other chair as abrasive, dishonest, and untrustworthy. You suspect that the chair of that department regards you as a competitor for resources, suspicious, and not a team player.

b. The dean used to be a faculty member in the Department of Hostile Takeovers.

c. Your department is among the most successful at the institution in receiving grants. Despite its size, your program received more than $4.8 million in grant funding during the most recent term alone, and each year the institution benefits substantially from the indirect costs you generate.

d. You are going to retire in two years, and the new construction will not be ready for occupancy for four years.

e. You recently received the department's recommendation to remain in your position as chair—a job you dearly love—by a single vote. You suspect the members of the department will blame you if they lose "their" parking spaces.

f. You suspect that, once the new facility has been completed, the Department of Hostile Takeovers will begin to eye space in your building as well.

Resolution

Although the dean's announcement is very troubling, you realize that you do not have enough information to make a firm decision. For this reason, you lay out your concerns as you currently see them, tell the dean that you will need to follow up later, and allow the meeting to conclude. After reflecting on the issue for a few days and gathering some facts on the size of the new facility, the amount of traffic it will receive, and its estimated date for completion, you meet with your faculty.

At the meeting, you lay out the information and concerns you have, present a few ideas, and ask them for their recommendations. Your decision turns out to be a wise one. One of your faculty members points out that both you and the dean have apparently overlooked a statute requiring that a sufficient number of handicap parking spaces be set aside for all new construction and retrofitting.

Armed with this new insight, you schedule a new meeting with the dean and outline what you have learned. The dean immediately informs the provost and president that there has been an oversight in their planning. Even though you were recently told that no additional funding was available, the failure of the institution to plan for enough handicap spaces "miraculously" causes new resources to become available, and the parking lot is enlarged.

Even with this modification, the parking lot still cannot accommodate everyone who works in both departments. You meet with your colleague in the Department of Hostile Takeovers and jointly decide to conduct a mini retreat of the faculty in both programs. Together the faculty members brainstorm the issue and propose a solution: physically challenged members of the faculty and staff will be assigned designated handicap spaces with enough of these spaces left over for students and visitors. The remaining spaces will be unassigned. With creative scheduling, you and your fellow chair come up with a plan to spread courses over the day more efficiently and thus reduce (though you can certainly not eliminate) the congestion in the parking lot at peak times.

CASE STUDY 6.3: THE PRICE OF POWER

You are the chair of a small department with only eight other full-time faculty members in addition to yourself. At your institution, chairs are elected, and the process of choosing a new chair for the next four-year term is about to get under way. You enjoy serving as chair, and you have let it be known that you are willing to serve at least one more term. As a tenured associate professor, you have a safe full-time position reserved for you, but you believe there is still much more you can do for your program.

One day, Dr. Conspiratorial, a tenured full professor in the department, comes into your office and closes the door. Dr. Conspiratorial states that there is a way you can be guaranteed re-election. Three members of the department are untenured, and Dr. Conspiratorial holds the elected position of chair of the departmental personnel committee that evaluates probationary faculty members and eventually recommends them for promotion and tenure. Dr. Conspiratorial never comes out and says it, but there is the clear implication that the three untenured faculty members have been coerced into forming a voting bloc.

"Their three votes," Dr. Conspiratorial says, "plus mine and yours— that makes five. And in our department, that's all it takes to secure a majority. By the way, if you ever say we had this conversation, I'll deny it. And no one knows I'm here."

You are shocked by this proposal but want some time to digest it, and so you don't respond immediately.

"Oh, by the way," Dr. Conspiratorial continues, "I think it'd really be great if you could find a way to schedule all my courses and office hours on Tuesdays and Thursday, upgrade my computer, assign me another graduate assistant for my research, give me a teaching assistant to correct the assignments in my courses, and set aside some travel money for that conference on the advantages and disadvantages of taking junkets that's scheduled in Honolulu next April."

You stammer out that you will think about it, and Dr. Conspiratorial starts to leave. In your doorway, Dr. Conspiratorial turns and adds one last observation, "Sure, take all the time you need. I don't think I'll have a similar conversation with Dr. Gullible—you do know that Dr. Gullible wants to be chair, right?—until noon tomorrow."

With that, Dr. Conspiratorial exits. What do you decide to do?

Questions

1. What is likely to be the result if you make each of the following decisions?
   a. You agree to do what Dr. Conspiratorial asks.
   b. You simply refuse to do what Dr. Conspiratorial asks.
   c. You report Dr. Conspiratorial to the dean.
   d. You meet with Dr. Gullible and explain what happened.
   e. You call an emergency meeting of the department to reveal what Dr. Conspiratorial has proposed.
   f. You call your attorney.
2. Is your decision likely to be different if one or more of the following is true?
   a. You have reason to believe that Dr. Conspiratorial is a discreet person who honors commitments.
   b. The vote for the chair position will probably be very close.
   c. You are aware, but no one else seems to know, that the dean and Dr. Conspiratorial are having an affair.
   d. Dr. Conspiratorial was your mentor when you were in school.
   e. Dr. Gullible will be retiring within a few years, and this will be Dr. Gullible's last chance to serve as chair.
3. Suppose that Dr. Conspiratorial had been a bit more subtle and simply made it clear that you could count on a lot of support from your colleagues if they knew that you were looking out for their interests. The implication might be the same but the offer and threat would have been far less direct. Would you then decide to respond differently?

Resolution

You decide that giving in to threats or offering bribes, no matter how indirectly they are phrased, sets a terrible precedent. You believe you would be held hostage to whatever Dr. Conspiratorial demanded next. Moreover, you would probably need to act in the same way if anyone else tried to cut a private deal. You meet with the dean and explain what has happened. The dean in turn brings the provost and the director of human resources into the picture. They decide to interview the three untenured faculty members one at a time to see if any of them will corroborate Dr. Conspiratorial's attempt to pressure them into voting as a group.

In doing so, they amass sufficient evidence to confirm key elements of your story. Dr. Conspiratorial is summoned by the dean and given a formal reprimand. The sanctions are that Dr. Conspiratorial will resign from the departmental committee, play no further role in the evaluation of the three untenured faculty members, be permanently banned from voting for or serving as chair, and lose the right to receive merit increases or inequity adjustments for five years.

Dr. Conspiratorial hires an attorney and sues the institution. Although the situation is tense for a while, the court dismisses the case as an internal matter for the institution to decide. Dr. Conspiratorial becomes increasing isolated in the department, stops attending meetings and social functions, and leaves to take a job at another university within two years.

As your institution prepares to undergo reaccreditation, the credentials of all faculty members are carefully scrutinized. One day the dean asks you to come to a meeting and, when you arrive, you are surprised to see that the director of human resources is also present. "I think we've got a problem," the dean begins and then turns to the human resources director. "Well, why don't you explain it?"

"As we examined the official transcripts submitted by each faculty member, we noticed a discrepancy in the record of one member of your department, a Prof. Plum. It seems that Plum was hired on the basis of a curriculum vitae indicating completion of a doctorate at Oxbridge University. Well, we discovered that we'd never received the final transcripts from Oxbridge, so I contacted the registrar. It turns out that Plum completed all the coursework for the doctorate, had a research proposal approved, but never completed a dissertation. Prof. Plum has no official graduate degree, not even a master's."

The dean then picks up the story. "Our policies say that we can terminate someone for cause for three reasons: sexual harassment, violation of our protocols for research integrity, and falsifying one's credentials. In any case, that part of the issue is moot. Prof. Plum is only two years into the position on tenure track. We're entitled to non-renew the contract of a probationary faculty member for any reason or no reason. The attorney says we don't even have to tell the person why we're not issuing another contract. I suggest you simply notify Prof. Plum that, after this year, there will be no further contracts and that the professor's services are no longer required."

Challenge Question: What do you decide to do?

Scenario Outcome: You are of two minds as you leave the dean's office. On the one hand, the easiest—and probably the safest—alternative is to do exactly what the dean asks: issue Prof. Plum a letter of non-renewal and never disclose a reason. On the other hand, Prof. Plum has brought a lot of energy to the program, receives excellent evaluations, and has outlined an exciting research agenda for the next five years. Besides, your credentialing body only requires college teachers to have eighteen graduate credit hours in the subject they are teaching, and Prof. Plum certainly meets that requirement even without the doctorate.

You decide that the easiest and safest solution is not always the most fair or the best choice. You meet with Prof. Plum, say that you were confused by what you have learned, and ask for an explanation. Prof. Plum breaks down into tears and says that the dissertation had been nearly complete, but then there was a terrible family emergency, the offer for this job came up, and before there was a chance to write the conclusion to the dissertation or schedule a defense, the deadline for accepting the offer had arrived.

"I'm not condoning what you did," you tell Prof. Plum. "You could have explained that to us, and we could've worked something out. At the very least, you're guilty of deception. However, you have a lot of promise as a college professor, and I don't want to ruin your career. So here's what we'll do. I'll place you on administrative leave for one semester. Finish up the work at Oxbridge and, if you do, you can come back the following term.

"Because of this breach of trust, we'll look at everything you do—grades assigned in courses, research results, everything—with the greatest scrutiny. But if you do the right thing and abide by every single regulation from this point out, I'll make sure that this doesn't become a factor in your tenure and promotion hearing. I believe in giving people second chances, and I'm giving you a big one."

After a distinguished career of thirty-four years, the last fifteen of which have been spent chairing your department, you announced to your dean and everyone on the faculty that you would be retiring at the end of the year. You have already begun the process of submitting the necessary forms to the Office of Human Resources, and you and your spouse have submitted non-refundable deposits for several trips you want to take as soon as the school year is over.

During one of your regular meetings with the dean, you learn several things that concern you. The dean believes that one of the junior faculty members you have been mentoring, a bright young scholar who has really helped your department grow, may have a difficult time during next year's tenure review without you being there to serve as champion. The curricular reform that you had hoped would be your legacy has been tabled by the university committee and is likely never to be approved since you will not be around to support it. Worst of all, the dean has canvassed every other person in the department who is eligible to serve, and none of them will agree to accept the position.

"The way it looks now," the dean says, "I think I'll have to merge your department with the Department of Abysmal Standards. I guess their chair, Dr. Narcissus, could run both programs. They're always under-budgeted anyway. Frankly, I just don't see any other way out—unless perhaps you'd be willing to put off your retirement for two or three years. I mean, after all the school has done for you over the years . . ."

Challenge Question: Do you decide to postpone your retirement?

Scenario Outcome: Your decision is made more complicated by those non-refundable deposits you have made on the trips you intend to take with your spouse and how disappointed you will be if your protégé is not promoted and your curricular reform does not pass. You are fairly sure that the dean is simply trying to manipulate you by the way the information was presented to you, but you cannot be certain that at least some of those undesirable outcomes might now occur.

As you reflect on the situation and gather information, you realize that what the dean has presented to you is a *false dichotomy*: the fallacy of assuming that the choice must be between two alternatives when other options are possible. Perhaps you may be willing to stay on as chair for two more years if the dean can figure out some way to give you enough free time to take your planned trips. Perhaps one of your colleagues in the program who was reluctant to serve as chair would be willing to co-chair the program with you during this period. Perhaps the dean could soften the blow of your delayed retirement by paying you an additional stipend for the next two years, thus increasing your retirement income for the future.

In essence, you have been given an important tool for your decision-making toolkit, as late in your career as it may be: never allow yourself to be forced into a false choice. People who bring problems to us are often guilty of black-and-white thinking. The very reason they believe they have a problem is because they can only see the issue as a yes-or-no matter. Good decision making often involves looking for a way to say yes *and* no or of identifying all those infinite shades of gray that separate black from white.

FOR REFLECTION

In many ways, it can be argued that *every* situation in this book involves a matter of making decisions. After all, when we hire a faculty member, evaluate a faculty member, resolve a conflict, propose a budget, or do anything else involved in the work of a department chair, we are constantly making decisions. Having a good process that we can rely on to prevent us from selecting options we will later regret can serve to make our responsibilities easier to fulfill and help our programs prosper. Perhaps the biggest takeaway we can provide, however, is to stress the importance of transparency in all the decisions we make.

Many times chairs will believe that if they reveal too much about the process they used to render a judgment and all the sources of information they relied on, they will be opening themselves to appeals and challenges. Nothing can be further from the truth. It is the chairs who give the impression that they are being secretive about their processes and sources of information who meet with the greatest resistance. Although there will always be exceptions, most people will be willing to respect your decision, even if they disagree with it, as long as they know it was made impartially and after considering other alternatives.

7

Budgeting

The responsibilities that department chairs have with regard to budgeting vary widely from one institution to the next. At some schools, chairs may not be involved in budgeting at all, except perhaps to sign off on expense reimbursements or supply orders. At others, the chair may need to develop a detailed budget proposal each year, defend it at a budget hearing, and initiate transfers among different funds whenever necessary. The key to successful budgeting at the departmental level is to know precisely what your responsibilities are in this area, whom you can consult when you have questions, and when critical deadlines (such as the last date in the fiscal year to order new equipment) occur.

In general, the budgeting responsibilities assigned to chairs fall into one or both of the following categories:

1. Budget proposals—Making the case for future funding.
2. Budget implementation—Tracking the funding as it comes into and goes out of departmental accounts.

There are several important points about these areas. Making budget proposals does not always mean requesting *additional* funding. Although chairs are expected to be advocates for the needs of their departments, the reality of this role is that it cannot always be about getting more. Sometimes budget proposals are simply requests for stable funding. At others times they involve making cuts in a strategic and well-considered manner. So the tools that chairs need in their budgeting toolkits involve not merely building budgets, but also maintaining them and, when necessary, reducing them in the way that best suits the needs of the discipline.

In addition, budget implementation does not merely involve expenditures. It also involves increasing income to the department through gifts, sponsored research, auxiliary enterprises, and funded activities (such as ticket charges for public lectures and other events). Too often chairs view their job as simply seeing where the money goes. But that job also includes considering where additional funding can come from and taking appropriate advantage of those opportunities.

CASE STUDY 7.1: USE IT OR LOSE IT

You are an external candidate who has been hired as a department chair at a university in a different state from where you worked previously and are approaching the end of your first year of service. In your previous position, the institution's accounting system allowed for "carry forward" funding: whatever you did not spend from one year's budget was added to the department's budget for the following fiscal year. You have been assuming that the same system exists at your new school. As a result, you have been cautious in your expenditures all year.

One of your faculty members, Dr. Zhivago, has proposed that the department sponsor a major conference in your discipline during your second year. As you worked with Dr. Zhivago on the budget, the two of you estimated that the conference will cost the department about $52,000 to host. That amount is significantly greater than the $30,000 you have budgeted for events. So by scrimping on certain activities and limiting supply purchases this year, you have bankrolled $28,000 that you believe you'll be able to carry over into next year so that you can supplement the $30,000 in your events account.

As the end of the fiscal year approaches, you receive a memo from your dean reminding you that you have a significant amount of funding remaining in your budget that you must either spend now or lose at the end of the year. When you call to investigate the reason for the memo, you discover that the state in which your new institution is located does not allow for "carry forward" funding and that all budgets must be zeroed out each year. You receive the memo on June 10, and the final date for all purchases is June 21 so that all expenditures can clear in time for the new fiscal year that begins on July 1.

When you reveal this new information to Dr. Zhivago, he is surprised and irate. He says that he has put a lot of effort into planning the conference and has fallen behind in his research and course preparation as a result. He continues that he assumed you had some arrangement in place

with the dean that granted you an exception to the state policy, and he
is shocked that you are only learning about the institution's budgetary
procedure now.

Moreover, announcements about the conference have already gone out,
and it would be embarrassing for both the department and the institution
to cancel it now. You explore whether you still may be able to conduct
a stripped-down version of the conference for $30,000 but learn that that
amount will not even cover the commitments for facilities and speakers'
honoraria that have already been made. What do you do?

Questions

1. What is likely to be the result if you took each of the following
   actions?
   a. You call a meeting with all the faculty members in the depart-
      ment to discuss this problem.
   b. You meet with the dean and plead your case, stating that your
      budget is bare-boned to begin with and that the dean's support
      will heighten morale in your department.
   c. You cancel your plans to host the conference and endure the
      problems that this change of plans causes.
   d. You spend the $28,000 immediately on supplies, equipment that
      is covered by state contract, and other purchases that are still per-
      mitted, and redirect the $22,000 you need from next year's travel,
      research, and equipment budgets.
2. What impact is this mistake in your first year likely to have on your
   continued effectiveness as a chair?
3. If you had not committed this mistake yourself, but it had been the
   fault of Dr. Zhivago alone, what approach would you take?
4. How do you go about rebuilding your relationship with Dr.
   Zhivago?

Resolution

Since you are a new chair and were hired from the outside, you were not
familiar with how budgeting worked at your institution. Moreover, you
received no training in how budgeting is done at this institution and so
were blindsided by a policy that you assumed would be the same as that
at your former school. All that having been said, however, you were at
fault for not finding out what the procedures were before making your
commitment to Dr. Zhivago and letting him begin to advertise a conference that you now cannot afford. As a result, you meet with the dean and
indicate how important hosting the conference is to your department.

You state that a lot of preliminary work has already gone into preparing for this major event. Since you cannot carry over the funding from this year's budget, you ask the dean to supplement the amount you will need. You state that your operating budget is small to begin with, and try to flatter the dean by saying what a boost this favor would be to the faculty's morale. You note that this request is a one-time event and end on a conciliatory note, saying that you are now aware of the budgetary process at the university.

The dean is no fool, however, and concludes that $22,000 is simply too significant an amount to bail you out. "What would happen," the dean asks, "if other chairs found out I did this? I'd have a line going out my door of representatives from every department wanting me to rescue them from their overspending. The system is in place for a reason. It ensures responsibility. I'm afraid this is your problem, and you're going to have to find a cost-neutral solution to it." Fortunately, you have been prepared for this response. Asking the dean for the funding is a useful initial strategy (after all, it does work sometimes), but you already have a Plan B in mind.

"What about the following solution then?" you reply. "I will yield my $28,000 balance to the college. Use it now to buy supplies and equipment that you would have purchased from next year's budget anyway, then supplement my events budget by $22,000 in the new fiscal year from the money you save. It's a win-win. We get the conference that we regard as important, and you get an extra $6,000 to spend on whatever the college needs."

The dean's attitude changes immediately from lack of support to admiration for your entrepreneurial thinking. "That's a great idea. In fact, I'll do even better than that. I'll split the difference with you. I'll take $25,000 now to buy supplies and equipment the college was going to purchase next year, just as you suggest. I'll leave you $3,000 in this year's budget to do the same. Then, once July 1 arrives, I'll supplement your events budget the additional $22,000. That way everyone wins even more. I get $25,000 worth of purchasing power for $22,000, and you get $3,000 to spend now, plus all the funding you need for the conference next year." That proposal is even better than you had hoped for. The two of you seal the agreement with a handshake.

CASE STUDY 7.2: HOW WAS THE CONFERENCE?

Two untenured faculty members in your department, Dr. Guileful and Dr. Selfrighteous, have both approached you for additional funding so they can attend a major disciplinary conference in New Orleans. Even though each faculty member has a $1,500 travel budget to use for professional purposes, the registration fee, hotel room, and travel to the New Orleans conference will far exceed that amount. You hesitated a bit in granting this request. The two faculty members have very different records: Dr. Guileful is a rising superstar who receives nearly perfect course evaluations, is a talented and prolific researcher, and is always the first to volunteer for whatever service work the program needs. Dr. Selfrighteous, on the other hand, is somewhat marginal in all areas of evaluation, and you are not quite certain whether you will even support Dr. Selfrighteous when a tenure and promotion evaluation is due.

After much thought, you allocate both professors an additional $1,250 from your supply budget to permit them to attend the conference. In the case of Dr. Guileful, you see this investment as a reward for superior performance, while in the case of Dr. Selfrighteous you are hoping it might serve as an inducement for better teaching and research. Both faculty members go off to New Orleans, and you give the matter little additional thought.

Upon their return, Dr. Selfrighteous makes an appointment to see you. "I don't really know what to do about this and whether I should even be telling you about it," Dr. Selfrighteous begins, "but my conscience has been bothering me. You see, once we got to New Orleans, I never saw Dr. Guileful again. I'm pretty sure Dr. Guileful stayed at the hotel and registered for the conference, but we were never together in any of the workshops, including the two plenary sessions, and on our flight back, Dr. Guileful was terribly vague about attending specific parts of the program. I know Dr. Guileful has a lot of friends in New Orleans—they were getting together for dinner and a trip to Bourbon Street right after we arrived and made it clear that *I* wasn't invited—and I suspect that Dr. Guileful saw this trip as just a free vacation."

You express concern and say that you'll look into it, but then Dr. Selfrighteous continues. "That's not even the worst part. You remember how the additional $1,250 you allocated each of us came so late that the Business Office just made out the checks directly to us? Well, I'm pretty sure that Dr. Guileful just cashed that check and used it for—well, let's just say activities that would not reflect well on the department if they were known. That's all I'll say." You realize that you now have a major problem on your hands. You did admit to Dr. Guileful that you were allocating the extra money "as a reward for superior performance" and did not place any restrictions on it. Nevertheless, the clear implication was that the trip was for professional development purposes that included attendance at the conference. If Dr. Selfrighteous's allegations are true, Dr. Guileful's actions may constitute fraud. What do you do?

Questions

1. What is likely to be the result if you took each of the following actions?
   a. You tell the dean, the director of human resources, and the university attorney about what Dr. Selfrighteous has said.
   b. You meet with Dr. Guileful and request evidence that a number of conference sessions actually were attended.
   c. You meet with Dr. Guileful and the dean, confronting Dr. Guileful with what you believe may have happened.
   d. You meet with both Dr. Selfrighteous and Dr. Guileful to discuss the allegations.
   e. You contact representatives of the conference and ask them to provide any attendance sheets they may have for the sessions.
   f. You do nothing.
2. The case study does not indicate the gender of either Dr. Selfrighteous or Dr. Guileful. Which gender did you assume that each of them were?
   a. Why do you believe that you made that assumption?
   b. Would your reactions be any different if either or both of them were of the opposite gender from what you supposed?
3. The characters in this case were given names that may have colored your assumptions about them. Did you find yourself drawing any conclusions about one character being "self-righteous" and the other being "guileful"?
4. Do you believe that you have any culpability for what occurred?
5. Suppose that, when confronted with the accusation, Dr. Guileful admits that Dr. Selfrighteous's suspicions were true and offers to pay the money back to the institution. Would that be a satisfactory conclusion to this case?

Resolution

Even though Dr. Selfrighteous has not presented you with any hard evidence to back up the allegations, you feel professionally obliged to follow up on them. You call a meeting with key stakeholders, including your dean, provost, a representative of the university's legal counsel, the director of human resources, and a union representative. Even though Dr. Guileful has had a phenomenal record, past success cannot compensate for activity that may actually have been illegal. Together the university attorney and the director of human resources develop a strategy on how to proceed. They have dealt with similar situations before and agree that the incident is no longer just a departmental matter. They contact the organization sponsoring the conference and discover that there were indeed sign-in sheets at each session. From them, it appears that Dr. Guileful attended one sixty-minute workshop each day and one reception at which food and beverages were provided. There is no record that Dr. Guileful attended either of the plenary sessions or any other parts of the program besides those three activities.

The dean, university attorney, and director of human resources meet with Dr. Guileful to present their findings. They conclude that Dr. Guileful has defrauded the university of funding clearly intended for professional development and issue a letter of non-renewal. In response, the union representative argues that the issue is not as clear cut as the university is supposing. There is no institutional policy about how many sessions a faculty member must attend at a conference, and the university has clear evidence that Dr. Guileful did indeed attend three activities of the conference.

Moreover, since the chair clearly stated that the additional funding was provided to Dr. Guileful "as a reward for superior performance," no expectation for attending any number of sessions was even implied. Faced with the possibility of a costly legal challenge, the university rescinds its letter of non-renewal and issues instead a letter of reprimand. The letter states hat Dr. Guileful exhibited poor judgment in requesting additional funding to permit attendance at a conference that Dr. Guileful missed 96 percent of and recommends against the granting of tenure in the future.

In light of this outcome, Dr. Guileful resigns from the department a year later. You are sorry to have lost such a promising faculty member

---

Your small department of four faculty members is bursting at the seams with more than 600 undergraduate majors. You have had to devote every available part of your budget to hiring adjuncts and professional advisors to meet this load, eliminating all the funding you once had for travel and equipment upgrades. Nevertheless, because your institution is highly tuition driven, you are under constant pressure from the president, provost, and dean to raise enrollment caps even more and recruit a still larger number of majors.

At your last meeting with the dean, you were handed your goals for the coming year, which set a target of at least seventy-five new majors each year for the next five years. You looked at the dean in disbelief, but your objections were dismissed with a simple "Just do it." When you show the memo to the faculty, there is a rebellion. They return to your office several minutes later with a document, signed by all three of them, voting to impose a grade point average requirement to major in your program that they estimate will reduce your majors to fewer than 400. They also have voted to adopt a department-wide enrollment cap of twenty-five students per course.

You quickly calculate that such a limit would not even serve the reduced number of majors that they propose. When you tell your colleagues that they cannot do what they propose, they counter by saying, "We just did. If you oppose it, the vote is still three to one. Are you with us or against us?"

Challenge Question: In light of the response you received in your last meeting with the dean, what do you do?

Scenario Outcome: Both the dean and your faculty have placed you in an untenable situation. The goals you were given by the dean would increase the number of undergraduate majors in your program to nearly 1,000. Even with adjuncts and professional advisors, you know that the quality of your program will drop precipitously if your ratio of students per full-time faculty member approaches 250 to 1.

On the other hand, the faculty resolution—which you point out to them is not binding anyway since the administration, and not the faculty, sets enrollment limits and GPA requirements—would make the program so small that the university would be more likely to eliminate it or merge it with another department than allow it to continue. You schedule another meeting with the dean, this time armed with precise budgetary information. You estimate the average increase in tuition revenue each new student brings the institution. You then calculate the net benefit to the university that seventy-five additional majors would provide.

You propose a compromise: with one new tenure-track line each year for the next five years, as well as an increased budget for temporary instructors, professional advisors, and adjuncts, your department can absorb an even larger number of new majors without harming the quality of the degree. You illustrate how the institution will be better off financially under your plan, as well as not having to incur the cost of the faculty searches to replace you as chair and your three colleagues who have already reached their limits in terms of workload. The dean promises to discuss your idea with the provost. Since that is the best outcome you can hope for right now, you agree.

but believe that, given the circumstances, the situation was resolved in the best way possible.

SEEKING EXTERNAL FUNDING

As we saw earlier, departmental budgeting is more than just a matter of controlling expenditures. It also involves increasing revenue, particularly in periods of severe fiscal constraint. The more entrepreneurial a chair can be about securing external funding, the better off his or her program will be. For that reason, here are a few revenue-increasing tools all chairs should have in their toolkits.

- *Grants/sponsored research.* Chairs with academic disciplines in the natural or social sciences are usually quite familiar with the foundations that offer grants and the strategies for making applications. Often these skills are learned in graduate school, but if not they are almost always developed early in one's faculty career. Chairs with fields in the arts, humanities, and professional disciplines may not, however, have a very strong background in identifying and obtaining grants. In fact, one of the most commonly heard complaints is "There just aren't any grants in my field." But this complaint, while common, is based on a misunderstanding. While extremely large grants are often reserved for the sciences and engineering, there are grants available in every field. If you have not had a great deal of experience submitting grant proposals, come up with a few ideas that you think may be worth external funding and discuss these with a grant writer or other representative of your institution's office of research or sponsored programs. While it is highly unlikely that there will be a funding source that fits your topic precisely, it is often possible to adapt the focus of your project to suit the interests of an agency or foundation. The key is to remain flexible and to take the advice of someone who makes applying for grants his or her career.
- *Donations.* Philanthropists have such varied interests that there is almost certainly someone in the world who would enjoy doing something significant to promote the work of your program. As with grants, you may need to be a bit flexible with precisely what will be funded in your program, since the donor's interests may not completely line up with yours. In certain cases, the donor's gift can be *budget relieving* and thus free up funds for other purposes. That is to say, a donor might not be interested in your idea for an endowed chair, but may be very interested in endowing scholarships for students. If your program is already awarding a large number of

scholarships, you may (depending on how those scholarships are funded) be able to use the donor's gift to replace existing scholarships and shift the funding you now set aside for that purpose to an endowed faculty position. The important thing in seeking donations is always to work carefully with a development officer: You do not want to secure a small gift from a donor whom the institution wanted to approach for a far larger gift. Securing donations should never be done independently. You always want to make sure the development office is involved in your planning from the very beginning.

As chair of the Department of Penury, you are constantly on the lookout for ways of augmenting your program's extremely meager institutional budget. One day, a development officer (DO) at your institution calls to tell you that a couple who have recently moved into the area, Mr. and Mrs. Opulence, were important philanthropists to the penury program at a small college in their former town. The DO thinks it may be worth trying to secure a donation from them to assist your program. You think that such a gift would be just the thing to fund the penury scholarships you have always dreamed about: a large gift would endow a permanent scholarship fund; a smaller gift would at least provide scholarships for a short time. Eagerly you and the DO schedule an appointment with Mr. and Mrs. Opulence and, over lunch, you outline your plan for a new scholarship fund.

"I'm really not interested in funding scholarships," Mr. Opulence interrupts. "What I'd really love is a splashy conference: The Opulence International Penury Conference! (I can see it now.) Tell you what: I'll give you $250,000 to put something like this together. Spare no expense. Book the best hotel in town. Get the best speakers. Let's make it the most lavish penury conference the world has ever seen! This event could put your little program on the map. I'll fund it the first year, if your department will commit to keeping it going from then on."

The DO is delighted by the prospect and says that the institution will look into it and get back to Mr. and Mrs. Opulence in a week. As you're driving back to campus, the DO says to you, "What a fantastic opportunity! Aren't you excited? What do you think?"

Challenge Question: How do you respond to the development officer and the proposal by Mr. and Mrs. Opulence?

Scenario Outcome: The problem with what Mr. and Mrs. Opulence are proposing is that this is a gift that could end up costing you more than you receive from it. You are keenly aware that your program is severely underfunded as it is. Making an open-ended commitment to a conference that will cost a substantial amount of money after the first year does not seem to you to be a very enticing prospect. In fact, rather than putting the program on the map, this gift could end up draining funds that are desperately needed for other purposes. You explore several options.

- Can you reduce the amount, sponsor a less lavish conference, and redirect some of the contribution to scholarships and supporting the conference in future years? When this idea is proposed to Mr. and Mrs. Opulence, they reject it entirely. "Either you accept the gift with the terms we gave you, or there will be no gift."
- Can you have Mr. and Mrs. Opulence underwrite the conference for one year and seek support from other donors for subsequent years? Mr. and Mrs. Opulence also oppose this suggestion. "Look," they tell you, "we're not interested in funding this program without a firm commitment from the department. You can't be sure you'll find anyone to fund the program in future years. Besides, we want it to keep the name Opulence International Penury Conference; no other donor would agree to that. This is a terrible idea."
- Can you charge a conference fee that can be used to cover the cost of the following year's conference? Since the first year is paid for, all the department has to do is charge a registration fee high enough that the initial funding will be replenished each year and used to pay for the following year's conference. A quick survey of likely attendees indicates to you that $750 seems to be the maximum registration fee most faculty members in penury studies would be willing to pay for this type of conference. You estimate that the conference is likely to draw between 400 and 500 attendees. Even at the low end of that estimate, the registration fee will generate at least $300,000, which is enough to fund the following year's conference and allow you to offer scholarships to your students. Mr. and Mrs. Opulence agree to this plan, and you accept the gift on this basis.

One of the faculty members in your department, Dr. Baiton Switch, has long been claiming to need a flux capacitor both for research and as a pedagogical device for students. Flux capacitors are so expensive, however, that your departmental budget has never made it possible for you to grant this request. You have urged Dr. Switch to apply for a grant that would fund this equipment or to seek some other way of acquiring this piece of equipment, all to no avail. You do not believe that Dr. Switch has even tried developing a grant proposal or a donor request that includes funding for a flux capacitor.

Finally this year, after still more pleas for you to buy "this absolutely essential flux capacitor," you have found a way to do so. You limited equipment purchases all year, called in a few favors from the dean, and finally set aside enough to afford the equipment. Just before you go on your regular annual vacation near the end of the fiscal year, you tell Dr. Switch, "Go ahead and order the flux capacitor. Dr. Emmett Brown, the associate chair, has signature authority in my absence. Get him the paperwork, and he'll sign for the purchase while I'm away. Just be sure you get it in this fiscal year."

You give the matter no more thought and proceed to enjoy your vacation. When you return to your office, you are shocked to find several purchase orders, initiated by Dr. Switch and approved by Dr. Brown. Instead of a flux capacitor, Dr. Switch has purchased two adaptive interface links and a dermal regenerator. When you ask Dr. Switch about these purchases, you receive the following reply: "Well, when I actually looked into it, we didn't really need the flux capacitor all that much. And since you'd already set aside the money . . ."

Challenge Question: How do you respond to this situation?

Scenario Outcome: You conclude that you actually have several issues going on here. First, Dr. Switch flatly disobeyed your instructions. You had said that Dr. Switch was to "go ahead and order the flux capacitor," not purchase whatever equipment was deemed necessary for the program. Second, Dr. Brown exceeded his authority in signing off on purchases different from those you had authorized. Unless you were vacationing somewhere without any telephone or email access, he should have checked to make sure the unexpected purchase requests submitted by Dr. Switch reflected your intent.

Third, you blame yourself for delegating authority to make such a large purchase to a faculty member and an associate chair at the very end of the fiscal year during a time when you would not be present to supervise the process.

After consulting with the dean, you decide on a plan of action. The orders for the adaptive interface links and dermal regenerator will be canceled, if possible, or the equipment will be returned for a refund. A letter of reprimand will be placed in Dr. Switch's file, and all future purchase requests from Dr. Switch will need to be signed both by you and the dean. You will also modify your habit of taking vacation at the end of the fiscal year and be on hand to supervise all end-of-year purchases from now on.

- *Concessions and auxiliaries.* If scientists have the advantage over artists when it comes to grants, the reverse is true when it comes to concessions and auxiliaries. Programs in the fine and performing arts have a long history of selling tickets to plays, concerts, recitals, and exhibitions. People may not think that a presentation by a scholar has any potential as a ticketed event, but in fact activities of this kind could well provide a source of external funding. If you have not worked with concessions and auxiliaries before, ask yourself what services your program can provide that others would find worth paying for. It may be possible for you or one of your faculty members to lead a travel program to a site closely related to your field. You could bring in a notable speaker, provide free access to faculty and students, and recover your costs (perhaps even generating a small profit in the process) by selling tickets to the public. Foreign language programs can offer modules on "Vacation Spanish" or "German for Business" and the like. In all cases, consult with your institution's business office about how these activities need to be set up and into which accounts the proceeds need to be deposited.

ADDRESSING POOR BUDGETING PRACTICES

When people in our departments either abuse their own budgets or make mistakes that have an impact on the departmental budget, we can respond in a number of ways:

a. We can view the matter as a *disciplinary* issue: "I'm going to fire Dr. Injudicious!"

b. We can adopt a *conciliatory* approach: "That poor Dr. Injudicious must need my help."

c. We can regard the situation as a *learning opportunity*: "Dr. Injudicious must not understand budgeting very well. I'm going to have to provide some mentoring in this area."

d. We can address this issue from a *problem-focused* perspective: "How can I fix this mess?"

e. We can resort to a *process-oriented* strategy: "How can I learn everything I need to know so that I can consider all my options?"

f. Or we can combine several of these options: "First, I've got to fix this problem. Then I have to make certain it doesn't ever occur again by mentoring Dr. Injudicious."

The way we respond probably depends at least as much on our past history with Dr. Injudicious as it does on our administrative philosophy.

In chapter 3, we saw a brief survey that the coauthors conducted of 351 academic leaders. A month after that initial survey, the same academic leaders were contacted again and presented with the following scenario.

In your position as academic leader, several program directors report to you. About three weeks before the end of the fiscal year, one of these directors, Dr. Profligate, comes to see you. "I don't know how this happened," Dr. Profligate begins, "but I just heard from the budget office that I'm about $109,000 over budget. I've got to cover this amount somehow, or I'll be in serious trouble. I may even lose my job. Can you bail me out?" As it turns out, this has been a good year. You have enough in your budget to cover Dr. Profligate's expenditures. You had been planning to spend this money on a number of computer upgrades, a new photocopier, and meeting the end-of-year requests of a few other directors, all of whom stayed within their budget. You won't be able to do any of those things if you use the money to help Dr. Profligate.

The participants were then asked whether they were more likely to help Dr. Profligate out by balancing the budget or let Dr. Profligate suffer the consequences in six different situations:

1. Based only on the information provided in the scenario.

2. If Dr. Profligate had always been careful in the past, and this is the first time in over a decade that such a problem occurred.

3. If Dr. Profligate had a history of over-expenditures (though never one of this magnitude).

4. If you knew that, during the past year, Dr. Profligate had been under severe stress from dealing with the death of a child.

5. If you knew that, during the past year, Dr. Profligate had been experiencing severe personal financial problems.
6. If Dr. Profligate had been a difficult director to work with, harsh
   with subordinates, and rude to colleagues.

When those participating in the survey responded only on the basis of
what they had learned in the scenario, they were quite divided in terms
of whether they would use the money they had to help Dr. Profligate: 54.5
percent said they were more inclined to balance Dr. Profligate's budget,
while 45.4 percent said they were more likely to let Dr. Profligate suffer
the consequences.

Those responses changed radically, however, when other information
was added to the case. Administrators became far more likely to want to
help out if Dr. Profligate had always been careful in the past (86.9 percent)
or under severe stress from the death of a child (100 percent). They were
far more likely to withhold help if Dr. Profligate had a history of over-
expenditures (95.6 percent) or was known to be difficult to work with
(100 percent).

The one added detail that continued to produce a mixed result was the
one about Dr. Profligate having experienced severe financial problems
during the past year. With that information provided, 52.1 percent were
inclined to give Dr. Profligate the benefit of the doubt while 47.8 percent
preferred to let Dr. Profligate suffer the consequences. What is interesting about these results is that, although they are comparable to those that
occurred when participants knew only the details given in the scenario,
the same people did not always answer the same way.

While 40.9 percent of the respondents always wanted to help Dr. Profligate, 31.8 percent never wanted to. But 27.3 percent of the respondents
changed their opinion from question 1 (the scenario alone) to question 5
(adding the detail about Dr. Profligate's financial troubles), *with the same
number of people changing in both directions.* What may have occurred is
that, while some administrators regarded these financial woes as a reason
for sympathy, others suspected that the faculty member may either be a
bad manager of money both personally and professionally or may even
have absconded with some of the funds.

In either case, what the survey as a whole suggests is that *budgeting decisions are rarely about budgeting alone.* Budgeting is simply the way in which
our values and decisions assume a tangible form. When we think a faculty
member is doing his or her job effectively, we are more likely to want
to help and more inclined to make budgetary decisions in that person's
favor. When we believe a faculty member is non-collegial, dishonest, or
performing poorly, we are more likely to be unsympathetic when that
person makes a budget request to us.

For all the claims we may make about allocating budgets only on the basis of institutional policies, we do not always act that way. In fact, we may rarely act that way. On the one hand, this common occurrence is part of what breeds cynicism on college campuses. How many times have you heard someone say, "There never seems to be any money for faculty salaries or anything else we need, but as soon as the president or provost want to do something, funding magically appears"?

On the other hand, using subjective grounds to make budgetary decisions is a natural occurrence at almost every college or university. As long as we are aware of what we are doing and why we are doing it, it is perfectly acceptable to let these subjective factors influence the way in which we implement our budgets, at least in those cases in which we truly believe that the department is being best served by the approach we are taking.

CASE STUDY 7.3: DO YOU HONOR AN ORAL COMMITMENT?

As the chair of a small department, you feel that you always have to work far harder than your colleagues to make your limited funding go farther. In March of this year, Dr. Hare, one of only four full-time faculty members in your program, asked you whether you could provide a little more travel money for an upcoming conference. It seems that, in June, there will be a meeting at which several important new developments in Dr. Hare's specialty will be discussed. Attending those presentations could be extremely helpful to Dr. Hare's research, and you regard your role as chair to be that of advocating for the needs of your faculty. Your budget is tight, but the fiscal year is winding down, and no new requests have been made to you, so you agree to provide Dr. Hare with what is left of your travel budget.

Now it is the second week of May, and Dr. Tortoise comes to see you with great excitement. It turns out that one of the keynote speakers at the meeting Dr. Hare plans to attend has had to cancel, and the organization has asked Dr. Tortoise to serve as a replacement—*if* the department can fund the travel. You explain that you have no funding left and that you have already made a commitment to Dr. Hare.

"I already thought of that," Dr. Tortoise responds, "and that won't be a problem. I called the conference organizers, and they're willing to transfer Dr. Hare's registration to me. Dr. Hare was going to drive, so there isn't an airline or train ticket to worry about. All you have to do is let me go instead of Dr. Hare. After all, it'll be better for the department and our reputation since I'll be a keynote speaker. Dr. Tortoise was just going to *learn* about these developments; I would be going to *contribute* to them.

Besides, you know I'll share whatever I learn with everyone else in the program anyway after I return."

You feel that Dr. Tortoise has a point, but you are uneasy about going back on a commitment you made to a faculty member. What do you do?

Questions

1. Would you make a different decision if one or more of the following were true?
   a. You had previously promised to help fund Dr. Hare's attendance at three other conferences but, for various reasons, had to break your word each time.
   b. Dr. Hare has been struggling to meet the program's research expectations for several years, and you had hoped that this conference would help get Dr. Hare's scholarly activity back on track.
   c. Dr. Tortoise were already scheduled to give the keynote address at another conference next November.
   d. You believe the dean may still have travel funding left in this year's budget that could supplement your own.
   e. Your department has a faculty development committee with a budget that is intended to supplement other sources of travel funding. Dr. Tortoise applied for this funding but was turned down.
   f. Dr. Hare will retire at the end of the next academic year.
   g. You suspect that Dr. Tortoise is actively trying to find a job at a more prestigious university.
   h. You learn that Dr. Tortoise either was wrong or misled you: Dr. Hare has indeed already purchased an unrefundable airline ticket to the meeting.
2. In a single sentence, how would you summarize the principle you used in making this funding decision?
3. Regardless of what the practice is at your own institution, if you had to choose only one of the following systems for funding conference travel, which would you prefer?
   a. Each faculty member is allocated a set amount for travel. The amount is unlikely to fund travel to a conference fully, so it defrays but does not cover the entire expense. Once this funding is used, the faculty member must cover all other expenses.
   b. There is a departmental travel committee with a set maximum that can be allocated to each faculty member.
   c. There is a departmental travel committee with no set maximum that can be allocated to each faculty member.
   d. You have a travel budget that you allocate according to your own discretion.

e. There is a travel budget that the dean allocates according to his or her own discretion.

f. There is a university-wide travel committee that reviews all travel requests and funds those it believes are most meritorious.

4. Which of the following two statements do you agree with more?

a. Conference travel funding should only be provided to those who are making presentations since its primary purpose is to encourage faculty research and increase the program's reputation.

b. Conference travel funding should be provided regardless of whether someone is making a presentation since attending conferences keeps people up to date with developments in the discipline, improves both their teaching and research, and exposes them to new ideas.

Resolution

You struggle with this decision because it brings two of your principles into conflict: as an individual, you want to honor your commitments; as a department chair, you want to advance your program by allowing faculty members to make presentations at important venues. You decide that your first step must be a conversation with the dean. You explain the situation, request additional funding to make both trips possible, and are told that the dean has no funding left to help you out.

Your second step is to have a casual conversation with Dr. Hare. You hope that, given the circumstances, Dr. Hare will be gracious and yield the funding to Dr. Tortoise. In that hope, you are disappointed. Dr. Hare insists that you honor your commitment and gives you no easy way out. "If you decide to take away *my* money and give it to Tortoise, I can assure you it'll be brought up at the next faculty meeting. The dean will hear about it. The faculty senate will hear about it. And the grievance committee will definitely hear about it."

You then speak with Dr. Tortoise, who is no more flexible than Dr. Hare. "Look, this is why they pay you the big bucks: You're the one who has to make a decision here. Which is more important to you? An oral commitment or the good of the program?" You leave Dr. Tortoise's office, smarting from the allusion to the "big bucks" you make since you know your salary is far lower than that of chairs in other departments.

In the end, you decide that there is no easy solution. You agree to shift the funding from Dr. Hare to Dr. Tortoise in order to support the keynote address. You also decide that, since Dr. Tortoise will be receiving additional travel funding this year, you will reapportion your allocations so that Dr. Hare receives additional funding next year. You do have to endure Dr. Hare's anger at the next faculty meeting and respond to a grievance (which is then dropped because you acted within your budgetary authority as chair). You know that it will be necessary to repair your relationship with Dr. Hare, but you believe that next year's additional travel funding will be a good start.

FOR REFLECTION

Even though department chairs usually have far fewer budgetary responsibilities than deans and provosts, it is important for them to understand where their departmental funding comes from, where they have the freedom to transfer money between accounts, and what spending limitations their institutions may have. For example, if you use a departmental credit card, there may be limits on the amount of individual purchases, restrictions on the charges that can be incurred for food or beverage, and guidelines for the types of charges that should *always* be paid by the card. Those rules vary widely from institution to institution, so be sure to ask a lot of questions if you have been hired into your position from another school. You may discover that what was required at your last institution is now forbidden at your new one.

Epilogue
Our Reflections

Throughout this book, we have tried to give department chairs practice in how to handle realistic situations similar to those that are likely to occur on the job. In reflecting on these case studies and scenarios, we believe that there are just a few final tools we would like to leave you to keep in your well-stocked toolkit.

- *Remember that institutions and departments are highly complex, inter-related systems, not mere collections of individuals.* In higher education, we become so used to encountering distinctive (sometimes even idiosyncratic) personalities that we come to think of our depart-ments as just random groups of highly talented individuals. While each member of the faculty and staff certainly is a unique person with his or her own personality and quirks, together they form a tightly interconnected system. In a system, individuals retain their independence even as they affect and are affected by other members of the system. As you make decisions, therefore, keep in mind the impact that any one action may have on others in your program. You will not always be able to predict all these effects accurately (that is what the Law of Unintended Consequences is all about), but you will make fewer serious mistakes if you adopt a systems approach to all of your decisions. See them not in isolation, but in terms of how they will affect other people, policies, and results throughout your institution.
- *Some of the biggest regrets chairs make result from their failure to ask the right questions.* The best department chairs are not always the people

who know the right answers; they are the people who ask the right questions. See your job as an opportunity to approach new challenges and opportunities with a questioning mind. Examine your assumptions. What is the worst-case scenario that could result from any action you take? What is the best-case scenario? What is most likely to occur? What type of precedent would you be establishing by deciding the matter in one way as opposed to another? How might your decision be viewed by someone who always tends to be cynical? Throughout your term as chair, it will be important to raise many different types of questions. Start asking them now. Most importantly, never assume that the best interests of your students, faculty, and staff will automatically be protected unless you ask whether all appropriate precautions have been taken.

- *Every story has at least two sides.* Many problems we face as chairs result from different people interpreting a situation in very different ways. It is common practice for one party in a difference of opinion to bring the matter to your attention, presenting only his or her own perspective in the matter. As tempted as you may be to do so, it can be highly destructive for you to decide on any course of action until you have gained the other party's perspective. Promise nothing more than that you will look further into the problem. You may well learn when you do so that crucial factors were omitted from the first version of the story you heard and that those factors dramatically alter how you will respond.
- *Developing and following written policies provide you with the best strategy for handling situations equitably and consistently.* No one, of course, can create a policy manual that covers every eventuality. In fact, policies tend to be ill-conceived when they are designed to address a single problematic case that is unlikely ever to recur. (Keep in mind Oliver Wendell Holmes's observation that "hard cases make bad law.") Nevertheless, there are many types of situations for which having a set of written procedures is to everyone's benefit. In the absence of these guidelines, chairs tend to make decisions on an ad hoc basis and run a high risk of setting precedents they will soon regret.

In closing, remember the oft-cited advice (attributed to numerous authors ranging from Mark Twain to Abraham Maslow) that "To the man with only a hammer, every problem looks like a nail." We hope this book has left you with many more tools in your toolkit than the administrative equivalent of a hammer alone. May you have nothing but success throughout your term as department chair. Feel free to email us with questions or ideas for further case studies. Our addresses are in the introduction. Meanwhile, happy chairing!

Appendix A

ATLAS: Academic Training, Leadership, & Assessment Services offers training programs, books, and materials dealing with collegiality and positive academic leadership. Its programs include:

- Time Management
- Work-Life Balance
- Conflict Management
- Promoting Teamwork
- Promoting Collegiality
- Communicating Effectively
- Mentoring Faculty Members
- Positive Academic Leadership
- The Essential Academic Dean
- The Essential Department Chair
- Best Practices in Faculty Evaluation
- Change Leadership in Higher Education

These programs are offered in half-day, full-day, and multi-day formats. ATLAS also offers reduced prices on leadership books and distributes the Collegiality Assessment Matrix (CAM) and Self-Assessment Matrix (S-AM), which allow academic programs to evaluate the collegiality and civility of their faculty members in a consistent, objective, and reliable manner. The free ATLAS E-Newsletter addresses a variety of issues related to academic leadership and is sent free to subscribers.

For more information, contact:

ATLAS: Academic Training, Leadership, & Assessment Services
4521 PGA Boulevard, PMB 186
Palm Beach Gardens FL 33418
800-355-6742; www.atlasleadership.com
Email: questions@atlasleadership.com

References

Birnbaum, R. (1991). *How colleges work: The cybernetics of academic organization and leadership*. San Francisco, CA: Jossey-Bass.

Buller, J. L. (2012). *The essential department chair: A comprehensive desk reference*. San Francisco, CA: Jossey-Bass.

Cipriano, R. E. (2011). *Facilitating a collegial department in higher education: Strategies for success*. San Francisco, CA: Jossey-Bass.

Cipriano, R. E., & Riccardi, R. L. (Spring 2014). The department chair: Consistency in a sea of change. *The Department Chair*. 24.4, 10–13.

Cipriano, R. E., & Riccardi, R. L. (Winter 2014). Thoughts on the chair role. *The Department Chair*. 24.3, 17–18.

Fisher, R., Patton, B., & Ury, W. (2011). *Getting to yes: Negotiating agreement without giving in* (3rd Ed.). New York: Penguin.

Mosto, P., & Dorland, D. (2014). *A toolkit for deans*. Lanham, MD: Rowman & Littlefield.

Orwell, G. (1949). *Nineteen eighty-four: A novel*. New York: Harcourt, Brace.

ADDITIONAL RESOURCES

Bergquist, W. H., & Pawlak, K. (2008). *Engaging the six cultures of the academy*. San Francisco, CA: Jossey-Bass.

Birnbaum, R. (1988). *How colleges work: The cybernetics of academic organization and leadership*. San Francisco, CA: Jossey-Bass.

Bright, D. F., & Richards, M. P. (2001). *Academic deanship: Individual careers and institutional roles*. San Francisco, CA: Jossey-Bass.

Chu, D. (2012). *The department chair primer: What chairs need to know and do to make a difference*. San Francisco, CA: Jossey-Bass.

Gunsalus, C. K. (2006). *The college administrator's survival guide.* Cambridge, MA: Harvard University Press.

Hunter, D. (2009). *The art of facilitation: The essentials for leading great meetings and creating group synergy.* San Francisco, CA: Jossey-Bass.

Leaming, D. R. (1998). *Academic leadership: A practical guide to chairing the department* (2nd Ed.). Bolton, MA: Anker.

About the Authors

Jeffrey L. Buller is dean of the Harriet L. Wilkes Honors College at Florida Atlantic University. He holds a doctorate in classics from the University of Wisconsin-Madison. He is the author of eight books on academic leadership, one book on Wagnerian opera, a textbook for first-year college students, 22 articles of academic research, 121 articles on higher education administration, and 114 essays and reviews. With Robert Cipriano, he is a senior partner in ATLAS Leadership Training, which conducts workshops for administrators all over the world and serves as a consultant to the Ministry of Higher Education in Saudi Arabia in its development of a region-wide Academic Leadership Center.

Robert E. Cipriano is chair and professor emeritus of the Department of Recreation and Leisure Studies at Southern Connecticut State University. He has a doctorate from New York University in Therapeutic Recreation, Area of Concentration in College Teaching. He is the author of a book on collegiality in higher education, three textbooks, chapters in three additional textbooks, and more than 160 journal articles. He has been awarded more than $9 million in grants and contracts and delivered in excess of 250 presentations in the United States, Asia, and the Middle East.